Rebirth I

By:
Jonathan

Rebirth I
Book Four of the Series *The Nine*
May 22, 2018, *First Edition*

Copyright © 2018

Cover Photo Credit: Adam Krowitz

All rights reserved. This book or any portion thereof may not be reproduced or used in any manner whatsoever without the express written permission of the publisher except for the use of brief quotations in a book review or scholarly journal.

ISBN-13: 978-1-942967-32-3

KreativeMinds Publishing
www.kreativeminds.net

Ordering Information:

Special discounts are available on quantity purchases by corporations, associations, educators, and others. For details, contact the publisher at the above listed address or the email address below.

U.S. trade bookstores and wholesalers: Please use the email address below.
email: publishing@kreativeminds.net

To my Father, through whom all things are possible.

Always,
Jonathan

Introduction

From dawn until dusk, generations have come and gone from this Earth. With every end to a great cycle, a generation is left behind and another is ushered ahead. The new destination is called Har-Magedon and is a place of new beginnings. To those left behind, generations will fall into darkness, an abyss of suffering. This will be a dark age for some, left to suffer the wrath of Satan's inequities. It is in this time that the words found within these Books of Nine must serve as a guidepost and a guiding light for those to one day find their way back Home.

Hope. Inspiration. And above all, Love. These Books of Nine are His Words transcending planes. Rebirth I (Book IV) through Glory (Book VII) are the journals I maintained during the course of this journey. These books are a portion of the Books of Nine that cover a period of 1260 days. Rebirth I began on November 25, 2011, concluding with the last day of my thirty-third year on Earth – which is alluded to in the closing of Book VII – Glory. The beginning will seem disjointed, but, as it will be revealed in the end, God's divine intention is revealed. This is the first book of my journals, the moments where God first opened my eyes and said, "Awake my child. We've got a story to tell."

Always,
Jonathan

Invocation

Blessed be those that read this book, hear the words, study its meaning, learn to see through the eyes of the Spirit, and understand the truth in these words. For it is not in the way most believe. And in time, the way it is meant to be known will certainly only be revealed to those who understood it in the final days. For there may be more days to come, another rapture after this time has passed. John said in Revelation 16:15:

> *"Behold, I am coming like a thief.*
> *Blessed is the one who stays awake and keeps*
> *his clothes, so that he will not walk about*
> *naked and men will not see his shame."*

In those days, only those marked of the Lord will know He has come. For all who remain behind and bore the other mark may never know He was ever here. And to those who wonder and seek wisdom, find peace in knowing that the mark is upon the soul. Find fire in the passion to receive a mark. Find faith that you are shown. For God as my witness, I swear upon this testimony that He has allowed me to bear sight upon each mark, their placements, and their meanings. To those who believe with their eyes, they will surely miss His signs. For

Rebirth I

the mark is unseen with the physical senses, viewed only through the eyes of the soul.

To some it may seem like a fable, a mystery, a story to be passed down from generations and generations to come. But to others, there will be truth found in these words. In hindsight, it is always easier to see. Blessed be those who may see by faith, who understand that hindsight will be too late. Blessed be. Blessed be.

Wonders (Part 1)

How do you tell the world that the words of these Books of Nine are the fulfillment of a prophecy that has stood the test of time? How do you tell the world that the seemingly inconceivable thought of how the wonders of the Lord became manifest in life will occur without the world ever stopping to take notice? Perhaps it must be this way for it to be in the way God intended. Perhaps for some, hindsight is the only way to understand. Perhaps for others, their hearts will see His Truth the first time these words pass through their eyes and waltz with their souls. For the words within this Book, and those that comprise all the words written through me, are the words my Father intended to be.

This is my testimony. This is the light that has been shown to me. I, Jonathan, do testify that the words herein are the unfiltered, unabridged words revealed to me by God, My Father, My King. The words are as they were imparted to me. This is the story of how I learned to hear the words He first spoke to me, how I first took notice and how He replied in kind, how unbridled surrender of knowing nothing became the root of being demonstrated through witness to a portion of All.

I, Jonathan, was born on May 9, 1981. I was born of normal conception between my earthly father and mother. My

Rebirth I

sister was born on November 9, 1982, exactly eighteen months after my date of birth. As a child at the age of eight, I asked to be baptized on Christmas Day. My parents had never forced religion upon me. I was allowed to freely understand Christianity on my own. Through prayer and the relationship I came to know with Jesus Christ – all through the eyes of a child – I asked Him into my heart in the fall of 1989.

During the fall of that year, I was riding with my family in the car, and though I must explain this portion of the story through the lens of my father on Earth, he remembers the day like yesterday. We were moving to a new town and as we passed a billboard for a church in that city, I read the service title, "If Communism falls, do we win?" As I read the words, I told my father that we had to go to that specific sermon and attend the church.

That Sunday my parents took my sister and me to the service at that church. My father can still vividly recall how partway through the service I elbowed him in his side and said, "This isn't about Communism. This is about good versus evil." He remembers those words so vividly and has used them in various aspects of his teachings. Following the service, I wanted to meet the pastor. Not long after our meeting, I knew that he was the pastor that I wanted to baptize me. I told my father that I wanted to be baptized on Christmas Eve of that year. As a child, I understood the greatest gift mankind has ever known was the gift Jesus gave when he died for our sins. On the day we celebrate his birth, I wanted to give him the greatest gift I could give – my life.

Wonders (Part 1)

Numerically speaking, the date of my baptism – the day I invited Christ into my heart – is a day that was a relative mark placed upon His Divine calendar. The meaning of this specific mark, as well as the reason for the emphasis of it being placed within this book at this time, will be revealed through the other sections of "Wonders" (which are divided out across Books IV – VII). But for now, it is important to just make a mental footnote of this relative mark upon His Divine calendar. As a child, I was being led in ways I could not put into words, but accepted on faith alone. At age eight, I made a spiritual transition similar to how the eighth note in a musical scale is an octave from its root. This was the moment my soul transcended spiritual octaves so to speak, though I would only come to understand the significance by age thirty-three. I completed the first seven years of my life as a child and in the eighth year, I sought a church and a specific pastor to baptize me. This is an undeniable truth.

As it has surely been surmised, my childhood was anything but typical though it always seemed to operate like clockwork. While I was not sheltered, my parents did instill the best morals any parents could instill in a child. As a complement to their servitude of the Lord's desire for me, I did not have a single drink of alcohol until the summer of my 27th year. And though these would be the years when I would test the boundaries of life while placing God on hold during moments of decision, it should best be viewed as a slight detour on a path of better understanding along the way to His intend-

Rebirth I

ed destination. In the end, I would return back from where I once came, with morals even stronger than I had in my youth.

    As I turned thirty, darkness would fall upon my life in a way that I can only describe as Divine intervention. It was a time of great importance in my life. It was a coming of age ceremony that I would only see in hindsight. It would appear in the same manner as how a surprise party begins in darkness. I had to experience the great letdown – the moment where all hope seemed lost – the moment just before a sound could be heard in the darkness from the rustling noise of someone hiding just out of sight. But that sound – that Voice in the darkness – alerts a person that someone else and something greater is there. And though it would take until the age of thirty-three for me to understand the coming of age ceremony had begun, once it was revealed, the divine ceremony erupted in song.

First Fragments

First Fragments is the beginning. This is how it all started for me. Sitting alone in a quiet, old house north of Nashville, Tennessee, on the day after Thanksgiving, I decided to give my cousin Bryan a call. Bryan lived in Rome, Georgia, and though we have always been close, the time between our conversations had always been measured in years rather than days. In what I can only consider to be the most suffocating part of my Genesis, I had reached a point where I had finally fallen upon my hands and knees and prayed to God for help. At that time, all I knew was that I could not make it on my own. I recognized there was something different about me (as well as my family). I wondered if others saw what I knew within. There was something inexplicable, where words will always fall short in describing how intimately the Spirit was alive within. And though I would not recognize the difference in any specific concept at first, I recognized it through the continual Divine intervention in my life. During the conversation with Bryan, I wasn't quite sure where the questions I was prompted to ask that day were leading me, but the academic part of my being felt led to understand my family's lineage with science in tow.

Rebirth I

In retrospect, the questions resonating within were prompted from the recognition of a light passed down from generation to generation; from my grandfather to my mother; from my grandfather's father to him, and his father before him. But this light would not have a name or an identifiable construct at first. In the beginning, there was only darkness and a desire to seek answers to a question.

In answer to those prayers, God surveyed my toolbox and through the set of tools he saw at my disposal, delivered a message so Divine that I still drop down to my knees in praise each time I reflect upon that time. The particular set of tools he saw and would choose to use as ways to communicate with me were a combination of technology, science, math, and reason. Even more importantly, he saw another resource in my tool belt – one I would never view in such a manner: my cousin Bryan. As he is for me, I am for him. Each of us can see a perspective often elusive to the other in the midst of God's conversations. We would not know each other's role at the time, but we did recognize a familiarity in spirit, a brother-like bond. To this day, my cousin is and will forever be a brother to me.

In the beginning, God's communication was masked in the mind of my ego as a quantifiable solution to the soul through sounds and genetics. At the time it seemed so simple: help me find Him quantifiably, so I can know what I am supposed to do with my life. But in truth, nothing can help a person understand what he is supposed to do with his life, for controlled decisions are of the ego. Following God's path is the

Divine plan. Complete surrender to His call and direction is what the earthly experience is about: learning to hear God's voice, to hear His Words.

It may sound so simple, but every person is like unto a baby born into this world, listening to the words of his parents, trying to decipher how to communicate. As articulate as the human mind can be in both action and understanding on this Earth, the sum total of this elegance is akin to a baby screaming at the sky, and mumbling some meager form of the vocalization of a sound to express the desire to communicate. Parents often cannot understand what the child needs, for the child doesn't even know how to express his feelings within.

It takes a baby months and even years to begin to communicate – and even then it is only through the most basic words. This analogy is as it is unto the most complex religion, unto the most complex science. This is the concept of understanding the idea of something greater unseen, though not knowing how to converse. For just as a baby must learn to observe the world, a human must learn to do the same – this time listening for God's voice, looking for God's action. Often a person must remove all of the noise – everything physical, biological, and mental – to hear the first sound of His voice. This is the concept of fasting. This is the concept of a sabbatical. This is loss. The sum total of this is darkness. For only in darkness can one learn to see the light.

It is said that the stars are always brightest in the darkest of night and the same holds true with the Spirit. How can a person know what he is looking for if it has remained unseen?

Rebirth I

In a city, it is nearly impossible to see the stars above. But on a beach of an unpopulated island, a great ocean of stars fills the sky above. The eyes take notice of this wonder. The soul stops in awe and becomes lost in the almost mythical fairytale of their light. This is the "First Fragments" of learning to commune with God.

On my journey, I was led to ask questions about the soul, about dreams, about a concept called astral projection. For some, the latter term will give rise to pause. For others, the words may strike fear. The unknown is truly the only source of fear. Danger is real, but fear is a figment of the mind. To begin to speak about the idea that the soul could be part of something greater prompts many to find rationalization. In fact, that is where I began. I accepted the possibility of the unknown, but sought reason to bind the concepts to all that is known.

I was led on a journey wherein I would seek to build a bridge between Eastern sciences and mediation to the Western practices of genomics, neuroscience, and biology. It felt destined that God was leading me on a path to understand reason wherein reason would eventually only give rationale to faith. It seems backwards, but that is part of understanding the whole. If a person is standing on the edge of a circle and wants to understand the landscape, he must traverse the boundary of the circle in its entirety before understanding what is within. For the soul is what is within. And all of the scattered fragments that help a person understand the soul are splintered in every religion, sport, art, science, mystery, occult, math, and language around the world.

With the only tools I knew how to use, I was led to understand how the controlled application of sound could place the body in a meditative state. I thought meditation would give way to healing and dreams – and it does, but the more practical understanding is that it is the point of divine alignment of the mind, body, and soul. It is a point where everything finds a state of harmony within itself and further exploration of the unseen can occur. The controlled application of sound was the equivalent of conditioning my body to recognize what it was already capable of, but first had to be found.

Again, this was a starting point. It was an idea. I thought I would learn how to control dreams and explore the taboo concept of astral projection. What I did not realize is that all of the concepts of dreams, astral projection, visions, and the soul traveling to heaven and back are one and the same. They are all different paths to the same destination. But, once the destination has been reached, the soul must be strengthened to fully understand the playground the child has found himself standing upon.

All of these terms and ideas are aids in attuning the body to higher vibratory states. It should be seen as turning a knob on an analog radio. Eventually a station will come into view. To someone without precise control, he will spin past the broadcasting station with only a glimmer of sound to recognize that something was there. Finer precision of the dial will bring

Rebirth I

the station in tune. But even once the station has been found, the mind still has to understand the language of the soul.

There are gates. There are elders. There are angels guiding all of the visiting souls. For some, they may feel Love and the mind rationalizes the angelic being as their spouse or someone once Loved on Earth. This rationalization occurs because it is the only way the mind can find reason in the inexplicably divine. The mind is assembling this knew experience and attempting to rationalize it. And while a soul may indeed interact with a soul of another from Earth, in the beginning, it is all a playground in learning how to see.

Eventually, with enough spiritual conditioning, the angels may take the soul to other destinations, but it takes time and commitment, practice and patience. Many will likely never seek to know or perhaps even become frustrated in the lessons. Some may get lost in the magic of "controlling dreams" (popularly known as lucid dreaming). It is the eventual understanding that all of the practices that help a person find a state of euphoria or bliss are attempts at finding this divine alignment. This alignment is the doorway to heaven. This alignment should be seen as how the smell of pumpkin pie takes the mind on a trip through the memories of Thanksgiving days with the family. Or how the aroma of cinnamon and nutmeg with a chill in the air may invoke memories of a happy childhood Christmas. The soul remembers home. It is that gentle tugging to Love within.

Though I'm sure the questions will arise, the experiences within were not induced by any drugs or stimulants. As I would eventually come to learn in my research, stimulants all affect the same blend of chemicals in the mind as the body is capable of balancing through practice and learned precision. These chemicals are important in helping the mind, body, and soul to align. It should be seen as no different as making sure the body has enough oxygen circulating within the blood – which is also important.

It would eventually become obvious that every stimulant is just a way for the body to regulate what it is already capable of doing – though the body does it best in a pure state in the absence of chemicals. Western science tries to solve biological problems by introducing chemicals into the body, and subsequently adding more chemicals to correct new problems created by the use of the previous stimulants. In the end, it is like adding cheap siding to a beautiful antebellum house when all that was needed was a good old fashion restoration.

So when it comes to understanding all that is written in "First Fragments," it should be seen as a baby learning to speak, even if it appears my human mind believed it was already strong enough to play as the franchise quarterback in a professional sports league. The beginning of Rebirth starts with a child miraculously asking the right question while maintaining a steadfast perspective to seek out potential answers through trial and error until God's voice fell into view. But God's voice would not be apparent for some time to come. In the beginning, science, technology, math, fringe science, and conspiracy theories were all tools used by God to communicate to me as he sharpened my pencil. And wouldn't a pencil

Rebirth I

be an appropriate analogy? For the hardened substance surrounding the central substance that can leave a mark upon the world has to be whittled away until the lead is revealed. And once the lead is revealed, it needs to be continually sharpened until the writer can use the pencil with the most precision required to create the most beautiful art.

So this is where it begins. This is the unbiased, unfiltered path, wherein God revealed Himself to me. At first He led me to His front yard, and then one day to His porch. After He watched me from inside His House looking admittedly lost, He decided to lead me to the door where I would have to demonstrate courage to knock and not runaway and hide. And when that day arrived and God opened the door to His Home and invited me inside, I understood it was never because I deserved it through my questions, my faith, and my perseverance. It was because I did not deserve it. In His Mercy that day, He said, "Son. Welcome to My Home. Have a seat." And, with loving arms, He held me and we cried together.

Every action I take will always fall short of His perfection. But it is the unbridled faith to move forward that found grace in His Mercy. The constant shedding of the earthly world would eventually be understood as His hand sharpening the pencil of my soul. At first I thought I was whittling away at my exterior to find Him within. But in the end, it was always Him. He was always holding me, when I was trying to hold on. In the darkness, I was cloaked in Genesis. "First Fragments" was an Exodus from darkness in the direction of a pinhole of light,

First Fragments

far off in the distance. For now and so in, this is how it all began.

...

November 25, 2011
6:00 p.m.

Well, this is the weirdest thing I think I have tried. Today, November 25th, around 6 p.m. I made my first attempt at astral projection. Not sure what to make of it. Here is how it happened:

After some research, I downloaded binaural beats "pure theta tones" through Spotify on my iPhone and listened through a pair of Sennheiser HD-280 headphones. I apparently attempted this for approximately 24 minutes. I began by laying back in my recliner in my living room and pulling a blanket over me (to ensure I didn't get cold since I live in an old drafty house). The lights were off and the house was very quiet, with only the sound of an occasional car driving by. Even so, the headphones muted most of it.

Having zero experience at meditation with the exception of some random yoga a year ago, my goal was only to achieve an accord with my consciousness – and not full astral projection. It was very difficult letting go of my thoughts, but I eventually managed to clear my thoughts by focusing on breathing through my diaphragm and focusing my thoughts on the tingling feeling I get on occasion in my chest. By de-

Rebirth I

scription, the tingling feeling is similar to how it feels the first time you know you've met someone that could become a significant other – sort of like butterflies in your heart and not your stomach. Anyway, the point is I felt myself plunge one step further into meditation and I began thinking about where I wanted to go. This was an epic failure and very short-lived (maybe a few seconds at most). I say epic failure, because every time I tried to induce thought into my meditation, it made me aware of my surroundings and I pulled myself out of the deeper plunge I had just taken.

Coming to grips with the fact I would have to "let go" of my thoughts, I plunged again. This time, I found myself having some upbeat music in the background flying by (or possibly on a boat passing by at a decent clip) several skyscrapers on the coast of what I firmly believed to be China. This lasted all of a few seconds when I thought "I DID IT!" Again, epic failure. I returned to awareness of myself listening to theta tones in my recliner.

Not content with what just happened, and actually unsure if I dozed off into dreamland or not, I decided to fight through my failures. I plunged again, a few seconds later I found myself in a group of people in a formed circle listening to a conversation. Everyone appeared Chinese again. Anyway, I nearly-instantly realized I was either dreaming or successfully astral projecting myself. Failure again. I crashed back to reality.

My body felt calm, but my brain felt frustration and determination to maintain awareness of this new consciousness-like state. I eventually plunged again – this time finding myself at first looking to my left along a grassy knoll – possibly a manicured retainer wall. I then looked right to find myself beside a pool with trees surrounding the opposite side. The pool had an older elegance to it. There were several people lying out beside the pool. Two girls walked by. My focus was on a lady reclined beneath an umbrella. She was wearing a 1960s-ish one-piece bathing suit. It was of a royal purple shade. She also wore a matching hat – very similar to the large "floppy" hats seen around Steeple Chase and other horsing events. She appeared to have obvious wealth and I found her incredibly intriguing, but not because of her beauty. There was something else of familiarity that I couldn't put my finger on. She was wearing very large, round sunglasses. I'm somewhat torn on her age because I typically associate that style of attire with women in their forties and up. However, the feeling I had was strange. It seemed as if she was possibly much younger – in her mid twenties, which would mean that this moment I am describing could possibly be from an earlier era. The vibe I felt in the dream was likely an earlier era.

While, I was able to assimilate more details and hang onto that moment for a few seconds, I again quickly became aware of the situation and found myself crashing back into reality. I sat in my recliner, eyes closed deciding if I had experienced enough. I opened my eyes.

Light flashed quickly in front of me twice – enough so that I had to blink a couple of times to make sure I was where I needed to be. It was the lights of a car traveling by on the road outside. I found myself sitting in the still of my darkened living

Rebirth I

room. I immediately jerked my headphones off and sat there gathering my thoughts. I felt dazed and slightly disoriented. I began returning a few phone calls I had missed during those twenty minutes and almost instantly felt an excruciating headache come over me. I hardly ever get headaches, so this was definitely unexpected.

And, since this was so outside of anything normal for me to attempt or even experience, I decided to start documenting it – hence this journal entry.

November 26, 2011
9:30 p.m.

I just finished a 40-minute session in astral projection. I did not have the same success as my first attempt. I repeated the environment from the previous night of a dark living room and sitting in my recliner. During this attempt, I felt much more of an anticipation and excitement as to where I may end up...almost like a child going to Six Flags. The only logic I have in my lack of success is the number of sugar free Red Bulls I drank prior to attempting meditation (I had 3 8.4oz cans). Also, I did not begin to hit a meditative state until I crossed my left leg over my right leg...which seems to be in contrast to the philosophy I have heard of not crossing body parts due to energy flow.

Now as for the minor successes, I did find myself again plunging into a deep state of meditation probably around 30

First Fragments

minutes into my session. I again listened to Pure Theta Tones. However, I have had a ringing in my ear that I also attempted to focus on "tuning" (as recommended in the Summun philosophy). On three or four occasions, I noticed several aural nuances. Prior to my body plunging into the next level of a meditative state, I noticed a super low rumbling sound – like a train in a subsonic frequency range. My attention diverted to the rumbling sound and I immediately returned back to my trance-like state, unable to achieve the deeper level of meditation.

Another nuance seemed to be a tremendously loud burst of sound in the 800-hertz range. At one moment, it seemed as if my high pitch ringing manifested into this loud solid burst of sound. I thought to myself "this is it" and just like that, returned back to my trance-like state.

As for each of the projections I found myself in, the first was a record store. I could not tell if the store was new, or old, but it was definitely a downtown business block store. I found myself in the back corner of the store with indistinguishable music playing in the background. The store was maybe 60 feet long and the aisle in which I was standing lead straight to a glass door that opened to a sidewalk and street immediately in front. I could make out other buildings across the street, which leads me to believe I was in a city. The store was full of record bins that could be thumbed through. I was initially thumbing through a few bins before I turned to my left and stared at someone at the very front of the store with his back to me in a black leather jacket, horned rim glasses, and some type of

Rebirth I

black ivy cap. A bearded clerk stood about two-thirds of the way down the aisle on my right side behind a glass trophy case counter. The clerk turned to look at me. We made eye contact and then I fell out of the projection.

In the second projection, I found myself seeing an image of a beautiful rolling green hill with a stream in front. The image blurred away into white emptiness along all sides of the image. I remember thinking about its majestic beauty and wanting to immerse myself into that image. I feel like I stepped into the image and tried to look around, then I became aware of what was going on and lost the moment.

The third projection occurred in a couple of brief, passing images. The first image was of an intricate crown-molding pattern with a scroll capped end whizzing by my face from right to left. I remember thinking "France." Then it was all black. A few moments later, I looked into the darkness on my left side, saw the off-white colored scroll end piece hurling in the direction of my face, which suddenly turned into three lights, the first stacked on top of the other two, but all of them blindingly blurred together. Then, just like that, it all went black. I thought to myself, "Was I just hit by a train?" immediately followed by, "I wonder if that is THE LIGHT that people see." Back to reality.

Finally, I had the briefest of moments of seeing (and feeling) my foot digging through wet sand as the wash of a wave was receding across the sand. I feel that I saw a brief glimpse of a child's face – not one I recognize. She had brown hair, smaller eyes than my daughters, and a really happy smile. I felt that she had a shovel in her hand, but I can't recall seeing it. As this image occurred, I thought, "I want to be here and experience this projection." Just like that, it was over.

The forty-minute long theta song I was listening to began to repeat, and in its few seconds of no sound playing, I realized I was in my recliner. I opened my eyes not entirely sure if I was dreaming in that very moment. I looked at my hands, and slowly assessed the situation. I eventually sat up and touched the wall just to make sure I was back in reality. I've never had to question my existence in reality, but for some reason I felt the need to in that moment. I did not experience the insane headache I experienced the night before.

November 26, 2011
11:30 p.m.

Well, I decided to make another attempt tonight at astral projection. Again. I think this was much of a failure. I still have not had the feeling I had from the first attempt where it felt as if I was truly in the projection. But for the sake of documentation, I feel that I should at least make notes of each of the projections. I should note that this attempt included listening to Pure Delta Waves instead of Theta waves. I was also lying down on my back with my hands upon my pelvis. My legs were not crossed. Each projection seemed more like a dream that I was watching. And much like my earlier attempt, I never felt the "plunge" until the very end of my session.

Rebirth I

Once I plunged, the audio began to switch tracks and I became aware of my surroundings. This session lasted about 45 minutes.

In my first attempt I was standing in the foyer to a public school. There was a white chubby security guard with her back leaning against the support framing to the glass doors that the students exit. There was a patio and steps leading down to where the students get picked up. The guard seemed to be telling a student [who looks to be eleven or twelve-years-old, African American, short hair (but not shaved), baby blue (possibly and white striped)] shirt not to leave. It seemed like they were in a spat over something. The child then ran out of the door toward the cars parked in the street. The guard yelled out, "Billy!" a couple of times but never turned to see what happened. I peered around the doorframe to see three vehicles. An older white/cream hatchback was sandwiched in-between two vans. Neither van was parked in parallel with the other car – it seemed like a sloppy job of parking. My feeling was that Billy got in – or was possibly taken into – the first van, but I did not see the actual occurrence. I also had the feeling that Billy may be missing and the back van was the one that was critical to the investigation even though the first van seemed important to me.

In my second attempt, I was standing at the end of a bar (which looked sort of like a Coyote Ugly). There were fourteen female bartenders lined up behind the bar, but not serving anyone. One girl, two or three people down the row from me, looked at me in a way I cannot describe properly – as if she recognized me, maybe? I cannot really remember her name, but I thought it was Brenna, Jenna or maybe Brianna. She seemed significant. That projection ended abruptly.

In my third attempt, I saw a quick flash of someone saying "I need to tell Justin about this." The voice was female and very distinct. She had a deeper journalistic tone.

In my fourth attempt, I found myself lying in a metallic, curvy frame in the middle of a green, grassy hill with a baby blue sky. It was as if I was taken out of a container. A round-faced, forty-year-old man with a beard and beady eyes said, "You needed to know there is another destination after yours." He smiled. That is all.

November 27, 2011
6:30 p.m.

Today I made another astral projection/meditation attempt. I initially tried to keep the same surroundings as my previous attempts. However, even though I was listening to Theta Tones with my headphones, I could still hear the sounds of my dryer in the distance. The occasional sound of the metallic buttons on my jeans clanking the interior of the dryer caused me to become entirely distracted. After about ten minutes of frustration, I moved upstairs and made my next attempt, which lasted approximately twenty-four minutes.

I feel that I am having a very difficult time allowing myself to meditate…as if I have some underlying fear of letting go of

Rebirth I

control of my mind. Based on my reading, this appears to be my "ego." It is not as if I want to hold myself back. I am mentally up to the challenge. However, some deep passenger within will not allow me to sever ties with my thoughts – if even for a few minutes.

With legs crossed, right hand over my sternum, and left hand over my diaphragm I eventually felt myself attempt to plunge into the next step of meditation. Each time I felt my mind resist. There was one moment where I was standing on a rocky path carved into the side of a towering rocky mountain. There were gates up ahead. Someone tossed what appeared to be a vellum scroll toward the gate. I was scared, and surprised that this just happened. I exclaimed, "We can't just go through there. We haven't been given permission." The shapeless, unidentifiable being replied back, "Just be patient and watch this." At this point I felt scared, realized I was dreaming and became aware of my surroundings.

While I did not have another vision per se, my body did eventually feel as if it fell into another level of meditation. This happened yesterday as well. The feeling was like my physical body was shrinking within my clothes. I started becoming aware of an aura around my body, which seemed to change the feeling of the pressure of my clothes on my body. While in this transient state, I decided to move my arms and see how my body felt. There was a small sense of weightlessness, but nothing tremendously different. I could visualize an energy aura flowing around my body – at least that was the only way my brain was explaining the feeling to my mind.

First Fragments

I decided to move my hands back and forth in a manner that could produce the "energy ball" that Qi teaches of. I honestly expected to feel nothing, but I began to feel a spongy resistance. It was very similar to the feeling of opposing magnets. When I moved my hands apart, I felt the energy ball grow. Pushing my hands back together was met with resistance and a squishy feeling. It did not take long for the ball to feel very large. Forcing my hands back nearly together caused the energy to eventually dissipate.

The next thing I decided to do was move my hands over my body – not touching, but a few inches above. It felt like there was a magnetic energy flowing around me. For several minutes I let my arms relax and rest against my body…only they weren't resting on my body directly. They were resting on about an inch or two of squishy energy. My arms were not stressed in recognition of the hovering position. In actuality, they were very relaxed – much like my hands were resting on a cushion. I eventually lost concentration and decided to remove myself from meditation.

November 28, 2011
3:30 p.m.

My attempt today around 3:30 p.m. failed miserably. I was very tired and felt like I dozed in and out of sleep instead of in and out of meditation. I attempted it for approximately an hour.

Rebirth I

November 28, 2011
10:30 p.m.

This was my second attempt at AP today. This time I lay flat on my back, head facing north in a dark room while listening to Pure Theta Tones. I was never able to completely clear my thoughts, which I believe severely handcuffed my attempt. Throughout the 50-minute attempt, I did achieve (what I will call) a "first-stage relaxation." I was able to eventually (albeit 30 minutes into it) achieve the feeling of an energy charge around my body. The room was chilly, but my body felt warm. It was a feeling I would compare to using icy-hot or a good facial cleanser. I feel like if this occurred in a much warmer room, I would have just felt warmth.

During this time I did feel the release of my awareness of my body. I felt what I could only describe as my consciousness begin to lift from my body several times, but each time I became aware of my body becoming tense – as if it was afraid to let go. Mentally, I felt less scared this time. I attempted to "roll" out of my body, but never was able to let go. I do think I felt my left hand begin to release from my body. I felt like I was moving my first finger and thumb free from the confines of my mortal body...which was kind of scary and cool at the same time. But that is all I experienced.

When I decided to open my eyes, I did have to check to make sure I was unable to pass through walls. While I am not sure what it will feel like when I leave my body, I guess it makes sense to check since I am sure I will feel as if I was mentally there.

November 29, 2011
6:30 p.m.

Today I spent one hour practicing meditation. Much like yesterday, I was able to eventually lose awareness of most of my body in the physical sense, as I lay there. Also similar to yesterday, I listened to Pure Theta Tones while lying on my couch with my head aligned north. As I lay there, I first noticed my left hand felt to be in a different position than my physical left hand. I felt like I could "move around" in both of my hands – but I was still confined and tied to my body. I would eventually move my finger far enough to feel the confines of my physical body.

There was one point that I felt like a force was pushing my left hand off of my body even though I perceived my physical hand to remain still. I felt a strong resistance by my body to let my hand be moved.

There was one brief flash of me sitting around a table in the kitchen of a beautiful home. I was talking to a couple of middle-aged ladies. One of the ladies said, "Shhh. Don't tell Jeff," as they looked across the kitchen where I assumed Jeff was about to walk in. Bizarre, but that is why I am writing this down. Of note, I never felt like my brain let my consciousness be set free.

Rebirth I

December 1, 2011
3:30 a.m.

Last night, I made a valiant attempt at AP (which is how I will abbreviate astral projection throughout the rest of my journals). I went to bed with the intention of keeping my mind awake. Maybe it was the Red Bulls I had prior to bed, but I could not go to sleep. I again listened to Theta Tones. I was able to relax my body and allow it to enter into sleep paralysis. When I swallowed, I felt nothing beyond my throat. There were multiple times that I felt my body dropping or lifting. A few times I felt an extreme pressure on my cranium – as if someone was pushing me down. Each time, I awoke finding my body to be very tense. I would try to relax, then fall back into deep meditation. A few times I heard a rumbling (it has been recurrent in each of my attempts). However, about two and a half hours into this attempt I heard a tremendously loud sound….like a train without the horn. It got extremely loud and I became equally excited about the journey that was about to unfold. And then, just like that, I felt like I had been punched in the face. No more sounds, no more meditation. I was wide-awake. I was not asleep prior to this, so I found the extreme exit of my meditation somewhat confusing.

First Fragments

December 1, 2011

10:30 p.m.

Tonight was another long, grueling session of meditative practice. Nothing seemed to happen though.

December 11, 2011

5:00 p.m.

I have not journaled much over the last week or so, but it is not for not trying to astral project. Since my last journal entry I have attempted to astral project at least once each day. In a lot of aspects, I feel I am getting better. At the same time, I also feel I am scaling a near vertical incline to get to the summit (e.g. controlled astral projection).

I am not sure if my mind is working for me or against me, or if any of this is normal. I have tried to astral project lying down, legs crossed, hands over chest, body in a star position, etc. Every body position seems to have its pros and cons. I have attempted it under covers, in a warm room, in a cold room, listening to theta tones, and also with no music. I have come to realize that warm rooms seem to help. Lighter clothing would probably be ideal, but it is winter, so I am stuck with the clothes I have. Also, my best AP attempt happened yesterday without music. It took my body much longer to enter into sleep paralysis, but I felt much more in control over my consciousness.

Rebirth I

In yesterday's attempt, I felt my body enter sleep paralysis. I was very in tune to my heart chakra as well as my throat chakra. My hands became immensely hot and my feet began to itch. Multiple times I began to hear a rushing sound. But, as I became aware that I was about to AP, I lost it. I attempted to project my energy into one spot above my head in so far as that I felt my consciousness lifting out of me. However, it was as if I was still permanently attached from the shoulders up. I focused, strained even – forcing myself to project out of the vortex of energy I imagined coming from my throat chakra. But, the more I strained, the more I lost control. As I type this, I realize that the previous sentence may be one of the most profound statements I've made. I will have to remember that on my next AP attempt.

To wrap up yesterday's attempt, I finally decided to look at my body during a moment I thought my consciousness was coming out of my body. It felt like my hands were about a foot off of the ground with the attempt to wrap my arms around an energy ball in a bear hug-like manner. When I looked at my body, my hands were only about a centimeter off of the ground. The rest of my body was flat on the ground. It was a surreal moment because I perceived my body to be in a completely different position.

As for some of my previous attempts at AP that I have not journaled, they are as follows: Two nights ago, I made an attempt to AP in which I heard someone tell me to "Come on" in a very happy and energetic tone. During that same attempt, I also saw a blinding white light (not the first time I have seen

First Fragments

this), but each time my mind began racing with thoughts and I lost focus. Unsuccessful again.

Last night I attempted to AP and felt my legs fall out of my body. It was as if my consciousness projected downward in my feet. The sudden falling feeling (in my feet only) caused me to jolt and come out of my sleep paralysis. During this time my mind was very aware of the situation. I was not asleep.

This morning I decided to attempt AP when I began to wake up. I have heard this is a great time to attempt AP. I listened to theta tones and rolled over on my side. I immediately began to hear the rushing sound that seems to be an entry point to AP during which I constantly lose focus. During the hour of my time attempting to AP this morning, I either dreamed very lucidly, or I had a pseudo-successful AP attempt. During the attempt I became very aware of a blonde-haired, blue-eyed face looking at me. She seemed to have freckles and pronounced facial features. She seemed very loving and attractive, but was not someone that I would have immediately pursued in real life. Her gaze into my eyes was mind-boggling.

Soon after her staring into me, I realized she was intrigued by my consciousness and that my body was lying down beside it. Now this is where everything gets a little finicky. Before I explain the next events, I need to explain some context to me attempting AP this morning. When I awoke and put on my headphones this morning, I noticed that I had several football updates on my phone from the ESPN app. The updates have a red and black icon and I usually think "Atlanta

Rebirth I

Falcons" each time I see it. Anyway, with that said, now back to my AP. When I became aware that I was being observed by a girl – and aware that it was my consciousness – I thought to myself "why not look around?" As I looked, I felt like I was in the Georgia Dome near the end zone with the Atlanta Falcon's cheerleaders. Obviously this sounds wacky and not in the context of an AP, so I decided consciously I was going to fly around and see the other girls. As I began to fly around, I decided to turn to look at my body. That's when everything vanished. I was in my bed. The original vision of the girl looking at me is burned into my mind and I truly believe this was my consciousness having an interaction with another. However, I do think my mind began to create the scenario of the Georgia Dome, etc. – which would not be part of a real AP – and this is where my AP began to fall apart. At least, these are my thoughts on what happened.

After waking up, I did look to see if the Falcons were playing at home today. They were not – so unless time travel, alternate universes, etc. can be a part of an AP, I have to conclude that the Falcons part was the blurring of a dream with an AP. I also looked up cheerleaders – just to handle my curiosity. I did not find one that was 100% the girl in my vision, but Elizabeth M was pretty close – just without the makeup as seen in the photos.

The funny thing is that I still do not find her gorgeous or someone that I would immediately be interested in. If this was a dream, surely I would have crafted a "girl of my dreams." And also, not knocking Elizabeth or the projection – they are both very attractive. I usually find smaller facial features more appealing. Anyone reading this will probably think it is distasteful or chauvinistic for even saying that – because Elizabeth is extremely attractive – but the point I am trying to illustrate is that in the counterargument to this being an AP, it would be a dream. If it was a dream, why did I not create a girl that I found more perfect?! Anyway…that is all I was trying to say. Both the picture of Elizabeth and the girl in my AP had very similar eyes. Maybe it was Elizabeth's consciousness? Maybe Elizabeth is not involved in any way and this is me trying to find some mortal justification to my AP. Who knows?…All I can do is document what happened and look at all of the details of my attempts as I progress.

    I did have one more instance before I awoke that I believe to be a very lucid dream. I was on a plane that was big enough to be a warehouse listening to a few guys talk while playing cards. There were some red and black chips on a makeshift table. There was some light gambling going on which I decided to partake in. For some reason, I was thinking roulette was the game (no roulette table anywhere around). I bet $5 on what turned out to be a card-throwing contest. I launched a Queen of Spades (very beat up and bent card) further than anyone and it slid under a door across the hallway. That is all that occurred. I believe this to be just a lucid dream – but at least I am documenting it as a precaution.

Lost & Unwritten

"Lost & Unwritten" covers a period of time from December 12, 2011 through February 3, 2013. It was during this time that the rate of conversations between Bryan and me had increased to a daily basis. This is the primary reason there is a gap in my journals. During this time, Bryan and I spoke so frequently that I mistakenly thought talking about the experiences with him was enough... rather than ensuring I wrote them down. Initially, Bryan and I each saw the purpose of journaling so we could make sure to talk about our experiences in detail when we had the opportunity to talk on the phone. But as time passes, so do memories. At the time it seemed important only in the beginning to write down everything to aid in recalling it the next morning. Only now is it easy to see that the undocumented experiences Bryan and I discussed verbally should have been just as important to write down.

During our conversations, our souls increased in strength and stamina, as did our memories and abilities to recall our newfound experiences. Bryan always had an eidetic memory and did not require as much need to write down the experience. For me, my mind is like a catalog of hyperlinks and reference points. While I may not be able to recite a memory, a movie, or a piece of information verbatim on the spot, I

Rebirth I

could easily remember where to find the points of reference that would re-trigger an eidetic recollection. So, for me, writing down the experiences was extremely important – especially if Bryan and I would not be able to talk on the day that the experience occurred.

In 2012, I gained a false sense of security in my ability of spiritual recollection. While I was noticeably becoming stronger, the strength would eventually prove only enough to carry me through whatever opportunity Bryan and I had to speak. We sent a lot of information through text messages or through social networks. The references in those conversations were always enough to invoke the most vivid recollections. We began speaking almost every day. And while the experiences were not occurring at that rate, there was an academic approach we took in our daily conversations with each other.

This time period should be seen as the adolescent years of our spiritual growth. We spent more time discussing theology, psychology, physiology, sacred geometry, and science than the big picture of the experiences themselves. Most of our questions to each other revolved around whether dreams, astral projection, and visions were distinctly different experiences of the consciousness. It was a valid question for our minds at the time, and no doubt one science will attempt to argue for some time to come. In hindsight it is now easy to see our adolescence, but it was necessary to understand how God was communicating with each of us. We were attempting to understand the irrational, when it would have been much simpler to just recognize "It Is."

Lost & Unwritten

And so as the year of 2012 passed by, my personal use of technology transitioned. I upgraded phones, lost my previous text conversations with everyone, and turned off my social accounts. Bryan and I talked more, requiring less recollection. In essence, this all lead to a period where the transcription of notes became lost among the clutter of life. Many times Bryan and I questioned whether we were being tasked with writing our experiences down – informally, or possibly for a future generation. Perhaps, more divinely, even as these words fill the pages of this book, I can now see how the experiences of 2012 could have been a distractor for some – inhibiting the journey to understanding.

In the beginning, there was a question and a response answered by God. While the journal entries sought to rationalize His Words through a masquerade of science and reason, the important part of the journey was illustrated – He communicated in the way we were capable of hearing, a way capable of capturing our attention, and drawing us into the story. For "First Fragments" was the unbridled truth in how it all began. "Lost & Unwritten" is a series of questions answered only in a way that Bryan and I could understand with the tools in our tool-belts. The notes on the handful of experiences I could still find, help paint a picture of the change in our perspectives. These are the days a shift began from wandering through a desert of science and reason, to hearing and following the call of God's voice. If "First Fragments" could be seen akin to Exodus, "Lost & Unwritten" was my Leviticus. For just as Leviticus should be understood from the original Hebrew

Rebirth I

translation as "And He Called" this is the time Bryan and I each heard Him call out to us in the wilderness – nothing more readily apparent than in the final entry in this chapter.

...

Early 2012

Early on in my efforts to understand astral projection, I spent countless hours helping my body find calm. And while it seemed almost impossible to do what I hoped to do, I continued forward. The idea that my soul could travel to places with the lucidity of the real world fascinated me. But as I got caught up in those efforts, I nearly lost track of how God was using my childish ways to begin communicating with me through dreams, visions, and eventually by allowing my soul to travel to the heavens.

Early on in the experiences, Bryan and I would chat about anything and everything that occurred. It wouldn't be until one evening in late winter of 2012 that something remarkable would happen. I had rarely dreamed up until this point in my life. In actuality, I could only recall a handful of dreams from my entire lifetime – but those dreams were special. Maybe it was a hint to the future that God planned for me all along, but those dreams each predicted future events in detail. Those dreams were not vague like the prophecies of Nostradamus. Those dreams were vivid and predicted something completely off the beaten path from anything that should occur in life, though the dream would come true the following day. I always tried to dismiss those experiences as intuition, or as an un-scientifically-proven advanced sense of foresight. But dreams were now beginning to become more frequent as I practiced meditation.

I never thought much of dreams. They were an afterthought to the glamour of astral projection. But the truth is dreams were the doorway that began God's communication to me. The moment that I realized the divinity in dreams was on a particular day in early 2012 when Bryan and I spoke on the phone. As our conversation progressed, I decided I would tell him about my dream from the evening prior. The dream began with me in a pool under a night sky. The pool was made of white marble or alabaster and there was a large mansion behind me. In front of me was an alligator. I was supposed to be terrified that I would be eaten, but I felt calm. As I recounted the dream to Bryan, he became excited and told me to stop speaking. He began sharing his experience from the prior evening. He was able to pick up – in detail – exactly where I left off. We traded back and forth with the experience until we found a variation. In one of our dreams the house was destroyed. In the other, the house was still intact.

It was in this moment that we realized we had a shared experience. Inexplicably, we both saw the same setting and had the same interaction. We had the same experience with the alligator in the water and felt no fear. We each knew in that moment that something greater than our original intentions were beginning to appear. We would not understand that

Rebirth I

particular moment as having angels guide us together for this specific journey. Nor would we understand the meaning in the details of the vision for time to come. But we would take notice that there was more than we thought we knew. It was in this moment of discussing the experience that Bryan and I would both lay down rationale and say, "Let's follow this and see where it goes." As it would turn out, he needed me, and I needed him. He is my eyes when I only have ears, and my ears when I only have eyes – and I serve the same role for him.

If our beginning could be seen as approaching His story from opposing viewpoints, Bryan was approaching everything spiritually (of Asian roots through martial arts). I was approaching the journey as a man of math, science, reason and analytics while learning to understand the Eastern mind. Science led me to this moment, though I never stepped away from God or Christianity as my cornerstone. Faith led Bryan in all aspects. It was through our experiences over the next several years where we would each traverse the circle we were standing upon in order to one day understand that whether it was science or faith that got us here, it would always be faith that kept us going. For Bryan, faith found him here, but the sciences helped him find reason. For me, it was science that helped me in, but faith would be where I would find reason. And between the two, we would walk past each other as we traversed the edges of the circle from opposing sides, never losing sight of the other, wherein one day we would come to see the view from each other's starting side. Eventually the circle's edges weathered away the illusion of us standing in two separate places on the boundary of the circle revealing that we were actually standing upon the same point, back-to-back, side-by-side, and face-to-face. For isn't that the idea of a circle? It is a point. Our perspectives were always the idea of looking in from the boundary of the circle's edge. It was only a different perspective until we would learn to see each other's perspectives as one, for we were always standing upon the same starting point, as is every other brother and sister of mankind. It was only when in this moment of recognition where the only words that could be said were, "Did you see what I saw? It was quite the view."

This moment was the moment that changed my life forever. And while I may use different moments with absolute truth of the same revelation in my journal as God continued to reveal more and more to me, I know that without that first shared experience, it would have been a much, much harder mountain to climb and truth to fathom. So if a person looks to mankind's books that seem to lack reason and understanding, the books that have not found a translation in the history of mankind, the books that may have pictures instead of words, or just pictures to illustrate words untranslated, know that those very same people who found reason to write the words have placed symbols such as these – the alligator, the house and many others – as symbols for others to understand their truth. I would later learn to see it all in hindsight. The more that is revealed each day reveals more about yesterday, and the days prior. Knowledge is the catalyst for hindsight, for the truth was once more prominent than it ever is today. And

Rebirth I

mankind's best efforts today have only further served to bury what was once before known. For as we find ourselves in the end of times, people may not even realize that the end has arrived. It is not a mortal thing, it is a spiritual thing. And these words will transcend this important time on Earth so that one day, others may know what truly was.

May/June 2012
Memorial Day Weekend

On Memorial Day weekend, I witnessed a friend receive a phone call informing him that his brother had passed away. It was a moment of perspective, where emotions were shrouded in the reactions of twenty of his closest friends watching the same event unfolding before me. When I returned home, I wrote the following words without any intention other than to express the rush of feelings inside. I eventually gave this letter to my friend as an act of comfort and compassion. These words would eventually go on to become his brother's eulogy where I was asked to read the letter during the service. It was moment heavy and without words. Below is the letter written:

...

We are all tangled in something greater than the mind can comprehend. And whether we choose to compartmentalize each major moment and the wake of emotions that flood our very being in the aftermath therein, or embrace the ride like a tumbleweed subjected to the desert wind – one thing remains true: Love is our greatest common denominator. That little four letter word that says so much in one short syllable – two consonants and two vowels – attempts to define an aspect of life that is truly inexplicable….the ineffable existence of our consciousness and how it resonates with its counterpoint in another. That harmony is truly rare. Maybe it is appropriate that the first vowel in that little four-letter word is "o" for it is the only letter with no defined beginning or end. Or maybe it is representative of a point so infinitely small, but so significant, as it is the definition of everything that is and everything that isn't. But, I prefer to think of it as a circle of resonance like a raindrop colliding with another body of water that sends a shockwave of vibrations outward from its very impact. Everything is disrupted and touched in the wake. There is no better explanation as to what Love is, than that.

And if that is Love, that is also the definition of life – the ripples that resonate through a person, a family, friends, and all those that are connected to someone who has left a resonance on this Earth. This past Memorial Day, I witnessed life – quite possibly for the first time without the blinders or shades that have historically prevented me from truly understanding everything around me. I watched as one of my best friends, and brother to Adam, received a call that no one ever wants to receive. I watched as 20+ of his closest friends all sat in silence on the boat ride back to the marina. I watched as many of them shed tears – no one quite sure how that moment extended to us – but fully aware that we were all impacted in that aroma of time. I didn't personally know Adam – nor did the majority of the people sitting on that boat – but we did know Josh. And to witness how Josh handled those moments and to realize the resonance that Adam imparted during his life – not only sent shockwaves to Adam's closest of kin, but to everyone touched by someone he knew.

Rebirth I

For those who didn't know Adam and to be touched by him through a degree or two of separation, must truly represent the force that Adam brought to this Earth. One raindrop, colliding with a body of water so hard that the ripples extend further than just those it initially comes in contact with. I can't begin to comprehend being in the situation that his family – or most importantly his daughter – will forever be forced to endure. And endure is an appropriate word, because someone so Loved and who brought so much life will forever and always remain in the hearts and minds of those he touched. The seemingly insurmountable challenge of taking the next baby step forward, having the next holiday without, attempting to somehow see beyond the void, the crater left in his absence – will define each and every person that ever knew Adam from this very point forward – especially his daughter Lydia.

It is those baby steps that we need to help Adam's family begin to take. It is the very purpose we share and the common bond among each and every one of us. Lydia has every amazing year ahead of her and should forever remember her daddy in the same vein that has brought us all together in this moment – to remember Adam as a blessing this Earth was privileged to have hosted during his 27 years. Please help us ensure Lydia will forever sustain that memory, and one day, be able to understand the outpouring of support from everyone that was ever touched by Adam's life. For it is in these special moments that Love and life are celebrated until we all meet again in the presence of the great divine.

Mid 2012

Though I have lost the original writing, I want to take note of an extremely special experience in the heavens. At the time, I was still trying to understand the difference between a dream, astral projection, visions, and the soul actually leaving the body and traveling to the heavens. However, I know now it is all one and the same. Each word just describes a different level of understanding. Looking back, I can now understand that it was an elder angel that spoke to me in the heavens early on in the onslaught of experiences. During that communication, the angel referred to me as a "starchild." At the time, the word amused me. In some writing I have run across, the term starchild is used to describe a person from another solar system. And though I had not read the word anytime recently, it is usually a word saved for those who choose to believe humans originated from aliens (or, more specifically, Pleiadians). Regardless, when the angel spoke to me, I understood a slightly different meaning.

The angel used the term "starchild" for two reasons. The first reason is the reference to light and how our souls are seen as twinklings of light to the angels around us. The second reason is that our bodies are formed of five points. Like a starfish, we are a mortal representation of a five-sided star. The angel impressed both of those meanings to me as she told me that I was a starchild, as was Bryan. I couldn't be sure if the word carried further meaning beyond those two, but she wanted me to understand how we each carried a light within, symbolic to a star above. We are star-children.

Rebirth I

January 2013
As written in Gravity Calling

"Seventy-Seven"

Eighteen months from the start of my Genesis marked the beginning of my Leviticus – the moment when I could say with absolution that God had spoken to me directly, not just in a way I could understand, but a way that Bryan could and hopefully others would as well. This was the moment "He Called" and marked the end of my days of wandering in Exodus from the darkness. The moment of hearing His Voice was the greatest moment of my journey up to this point. On an evening in January, Bryan and I had increased our conversations to multiple times a week with each call generally lasting a couple of hours. Our original intention of understanding dreams had fully transitioned to understanding how God was working in our lives and communicating with us through visions and the world around us. By this point, we had each experienced multiple angelic encounters and had each heard the voice of God. However, we were still searching to understand the chasm between the spiritual and earthly worlds – how to bridge the two worlds as one.

Over the previous months we had begun to realize that our conversations on the phone were as significant as prayer. We came to understand that when souls were driving conversation, God was listening and would respond in ways we would be able to understand. There were numerous phone calls when we would discuss a particular topic and then a seemingly improbable answer would manifest in our earthly walks over the course of the following days. Though it took the discernible eye of the spirit, we noticed and made sure to discuss the occurrences. It was still somewhat hard for us to fully accept by faith alone (without a smidgen of doubt entering the equation) that these occurrences were not our own interpretations used to support our spiritual desires. But, we ventured on. And perhaps the fact we always humbly raised questions instead of formed answers to what we thought we observed was the impetus behind God's grand intervention to come.

Throughout Bryan's and my random banter during our conversations, we began to call these perceived call-and-response moments between God and our conversations "seven-and-seven moments," which represented a spiritual high-five of sorts. These seven and seven moments could come in the form of a vision one of us had and an experience the other had that supported the other. They could come as shared visions, or even as a moment where God imparted something in a vision that would foreshadow the rise of an earthly equivalent in the following days. It could come from a prayer request and a perceived answer. We took comfort that God was throwing out "atta-boys" to help each of us build confidence in our walks. The use of the term "seven-and-seven moment" at this point in our conversation was so commonplace and frequent, we even joked about it becoming mildly off-putting in the midst of conversation.

Rebirth I

So, on that particular evening in January, Bryan and I were talking about money and windfalls. For me, it was the first time I had discussed my thoughts on money after my financial collapse. I had come to learn that everything that enters into our lives is done so by God's hand. We only have one purpose, and that is to serve Him in the manner He has chosen for us. Along the journey, He provides us the resources we need to find peace and continue onward. As long as we understand and observe that everything is given to us from Him as a vehicle purposed for His divine intention and not earned by our egoic desires, it becomes easier to see there is no need for any material items in our lives. As I discussed these thoughts with Bryan, I made a specific reference to winning the lottery or finding a random sack of money sitting on your doorstep. For most, they would take the money and squander it, or perhaps invest it. Some may even use it for good, but still take a portion for themselves But in this conversation, I made it clear that if something like this were ever to be placed randomly into my life with no apparent spiritual impetus, I could not take one single dollar from the amount to benefit myself. I would not pay off any of the debt that still hung over my head, for it was debt I had accrued while my ego was driving, and it was upon me to make good on the financial damage I had allowed my ego to create. Instead, I would deliver the full amount of money in whatever manner God directed me to do.

Our conversation ended on a very high spiritual note. We said our goodbyes and I went to bed. The next morning I awoke feeling extremely refreshed. The morning had an air of certainty, resolve and peace. It was a rare morning that I got ready early before work and was able to relax to some music and meditate before leaving my place. But when the time came to leave, I could never have been prepared for what was to come. As I opened my door to the open-air breezeway that separated the other seven units or so in my building, I looked down before me and saw a bundle of cash sitting on my doorstep. Clearly it was possible that it fell out of someone's pocket, but the bundle was wadded up into nearly the size of a softball. I looked down either side of my hallway. I walked to the stairwell and elevator. I looked in the parking lot. It was clear that no one was recently around that would have dropped it. I picked it up and began to think about the conversation I had with Bryan the previous evening. I stood there in disbelief that a message from God would be so overtly direct in response to the conversation. To this point, any seven and seven moments that Bryan and I had experienced could be left unto interpretation. But this was just the start. (To dispel any doubt for the reader, it is important to understand that Bryan lives four hours away. We also took these types of events very seriously as well – never joking about the gravity they held).

I walked down to my Jeep, careful to make sure if I saw someone leaving to ask them if they had lost any money. No one was around. When I reached my Jeep, I sat down and unwadded the bills to count the amount I held in my hand. It became apparent there were a lot of smaller denominations that made the bundle appear larger in size, but as I arrived at the final total my jaw hit the ground. I was holding seventy-

Rebirth I

seven dollars. I immediately sent Bryan a picture with no context behind the image. He initially thought I was joking with him and called me back immediately to understand what I had found. If there was ever a moment that God disambiguated all of the moments we thought had potentially occurred in our pasts, this was the moment.

But this was just the start of a spiritual test. In truth, $77 is a small amount of money for most people, easily lost in the shuffle of the busy world. But, with this $77, I was now tasked with walking the walk from the conversation the night prior. I was in no rush to make a decision. Instead, I chose to hold onto the cash until I could identify God leading me in a direction. As divine circumstances would have it (and I would only recognize the timing in retrospect days later), on the evening of the seventh day from the original conversation with Bryan, I would see a friend's post (her name is Leah) on a social network. Leah's message was asking for people to help contribute any way they could to help a family she knew rebuild their life after having their house completely destroyed by fire. The following morning – the seventh day from when I found the bundle of money – I would write a divinely inspired letter and deliver it in an unmarked envelope along with the $77 to Leah, so that she could deliver it to her friend. The timing of it all was again, another seven and seven moment that I would only see in hindsight of my actions. And while $77 may not seem like much to help someone who has just lost everything, the last paragraph of the letter hopefully sums up the impetus behind the letter and God's intention in my action.

Lost & Unwritten

This experience and letter marked the beginning of my Leviticus and my second understanding of the divine language of life, loss, and Love. The letter is included below:

...

 Some say strange things "just happen" but I'm a firm believer in everything having a purpose. Even the seemingly most insignificant things have the potential to play a much more important role in the master plan. Nothing could exemplify this better for me than what occurred the morning of January 18th. But to understand the 18th, let's first rewind to the evening of the 17th.

 On the evening of the 17th I was having a philosophical, theological and spiritual discussion with a close friend. During that conversation, we spoke in depth about how our Creator is always guiding us – granting us the decision to acknowledge and follow His leads through life. His "leads" may not come in the forms of answers or guidance we expect to see and therefore most do not understand how to truly experience the walk within their own faith. Most people expect when they ask for _____ , the only answer is to receive exactly what they asked for. To most, anything less cannot be divine or the product of His doing. The misnomer is in the most obvious flaw – that flaw is that we have no right to ask for anything. We have already been given everything. And within that space, we serve as vessels for our Creator – to follow the leads He has set forth and be able to positively share His intention within that space.

 I could go off into a tangent about how egos and earthly perceptions cloud our understanding of the marvelous leads that are constantly set forth before us, but I'll save that discussion for a later time. The important part I want to communicate is the main topic of the conversation from the evening of the 17th – which is also why I am writing you this letter.

Rebirth I

During that conversation, my friend and I spoke at great length about the people who ask God for money or wealth, and believe their prayers go unanswered (pretty much, this was the focal point of the conversation). Truthfully, most people believe that only they can manufacture their own wealth and God won't answer the "please let me win the lottery" prayer. But the main point of our discussion was that most people won't acknowledge when God bestows an opportunity to do great things with what he has given – regardless of our perception of the significance, because definitions of significance vary from person to person. A boat to one person is a yacht to another – or that very boat could mean an opportunity to feed a family. Perception is all in the eye of the beholder. Within the context of our conversation, we discussed how "windfalls" of income shouldn't have a defined set of zeros attached to it. Nor should a "windfall" have to be delivered in expected mechanisms such as winning the lottery, receiving an inheritance, or (and this next part is important) finding a sack of money at your front door.

The conversation could not have had a greater stamp of His approval than what occurred the morning of the 18th. As I rushed out the door to go to work, I opened the door and there in front of me, in the midst of the highly trafficked hallway of my condo complex, was a wadded up bundle of cash. I looked around thinking it was a joke at first. But as I realized no one was (or had been) recently around and this money was clearly in front of me and intended for my eyes, this was God's acknowledgement of my prior night's conversation. Within this moment was the opportunity for me to demonstrate that I could mean the words I had spoken the previous night.

While the amount of cash may not seem significant, therein lies a greater acknowledgement. The amount was $77. For anyone familiar with *the numeric significance within the evolution of humanity, that person would easily be able to acknowledge the number 7 has always carried a divine significance. It is a spiritual number of sorts. Now I could again digress on topics of the history of linguistics and how language evolved around the world and how numbers were initially formed, but that could be a book in and of itself. For now, please trust in me when I say that the number 77 carries a far greater significance in our earthly and spiritual journey than most people will ever realize. Basically, this was God communicating with me on terms that I could clearly and unmistakably understand. For someone else, it may have been another method. For me, in this moment, I heard everything He was saying.*

I acknowledged that this $77 represented a far greater purpose than I could understand. Several days passed with no signs of what to do. I wasn't actively looking, nor was I anxious to make an irrational decision. I knew that somehow passively, I would be able to be a vessel for his intention. So it came as no surprise that a very dear friend, Leah, posted on Facebook a brief story about your situation and how we could all help. I knew in that very moment that I had the full acknowledgement of God's intention with the small "windfall" outside of my door.

Perhaps the $77 may not mean anything to you directly. Perhaps it will be able to be used with the medical costs. Perhaps the intention was not in the $77 itself, but to acknowledge that God somehow foresaw the events occurring in your family's life and also foresaw the amount of Love that would be spilled forth among friends, family and even those just touched by your situation. Perhaps, the $77 is just God saying "I'm here" and maybe that is the most important point of all of this. I can't be entirely certain of His intention of this $77 for you, but I hope that somehow

Rebirth I

within the money, the story, or somewhere in between, that you can find peace, trust and faith in Our Creator.

- Warmest Blessings -

...

The Written

"The Written" is the portion of the journey from when I first heard God's voice emphatically in the world around me to the days that would run through my journey into the desert. The steps into the sands of the desert should be seen as my Numbers, marked near the ending of "The Written" and the beginning of "First Revelation."

This is the time when Bryan and I took notice of God's Divine work and understood His intentions for each of us to write about our experiences. Though the reason for writing is not clarified within the writing itself, our understanding came from the many conversations and responses that God provided to us. How we arrived at this place is not relevant. The relevance that should be understood is that we did indeed arrive at this place. If by nothing else, it was through faith alone.

To hear His Voice cry out in the wilderness is indescribable. The words that are written in these books will never do the experience justice. When I look back on that day, all I can think about is how amazing it was, and how amazing it became. This was uncharted territory – an adventure into the unknown. As our strength in our spiritual eyes and ears grew, so did His lessons. Each one built upon the previous one until

Rebirth I

there was a point that became clearly defined in hindsight, though hard to see as it occurred.

These were the days of forever just beginning – a lifetime of ever-after, wrapped up in His Divine packaging. Though the words written begin as seen through the eyes of a child, the more that time passed, the older the perspective became. These are the days a child learns how to walk on his own, and when a parent has to watch as the child stumbles and falls. But it is important to understand that when a child falls down, the parent is there to help him back up until he can learn to stand back up on his own. These were the days of defining moments – the moments that God stretched the bounds of first faith found. These are the days that God started leading a child in His direction, calling him to His home. It is more than words and conquering the fear of the unknown. These were the days that second faith was born.

...

February 4, 2013

Today's experience was similar to how I witnessed the $77 manifest from words into reality just days prior. Today I was having lunch with Andrew – a friend that has recently fallen more into view as we each journey along our spiritual paths. As we had a conversation over coffee, I started explaining to him just the highlights from my journey. Until this day, I had not shared any of the experiences with anyone other than Brian and Sam from work. So, as we talked, I started to share with him the story of the $77. As I did, my phone vibrated with a message.

The message was from my ex-wife's brother. I had not spoken to him in years. As I noticed how "out of place" it seemed, I shared with Andrew that this could be another example similar to the $77. Sure enough, the message read:

*"Hey man, I know it's been along time.
Hope all is well. I woke up this morning and
just had this feeling I needed to reach
out to ya. No matter what roads we go down
you'll always be a brother to me.
I'm sorry for losing contact with you for so long"*

And while some people may chalk up the message as coincidence, the perception of seeing how God began speaking to me by placing "out of place" experiences into my daily walk began to unfold. The message made for an even more enlightened conversation with Andrew. Perhaps the message was partly for me, perhaps it was partly for Andrew to see.

February 17, 2013

Bryan was shared the following message from an angel this morning: "Magic is fuel for the ego, glitter for the igno-

Rebirth I

rant, but unyielding faith and Love will take you across the universe and back."

February 18, 2013

The experience began with the notation of a college class numbering system. I understood that I had missed an "010 history lesson" that revealed what was driving the world to destruction. Someone was destroying the world from each direction. Four of five directions had already been destroyed. I stood in the fifth. It seemed I was observing the White House with a cave below. I was in this experience's role with a brother. A sniper was firing upon everyone. In our view, there was a new multi-story building on a street corner with green grass and wrought-iron fencing in front. There were armed guards everywhere. I was constantly asked by someone unseen "what the mind of the killer was." After the chaos subsided, I found my brother, who was saying I missed the history lesson. He chimed in and told me it had to do with Thomas _____. I am unsure of the last name given.

People kept dying. There was a crazy guy who acknowledged me in the moment. He had hacked every Android phone. He attached two nuclear missiles to a drone-like craft on which we flew. It was important to him that both bombs went off over densely populated areas. The bombs had social network labels – Twitter was one of them. I told the US government I was truly scared for humanity because this was the beginning of the end. I watched as a drone with two missiles attached to the craft morphed into two meteors with the power of a million tons of destruction.

I was taken from a skyscraper rooftop to witness the events back to the ground. I felt like it was necessary in the destroyer's eyes that humanity lost millions of lives. The government pushed me to answer why only Android devices were hacked. I could only rationalize the answer to be because "it was easy" and "it would drive others to move to iPhones." I also thought the initiative was backed by a corporation and the feedback was going to backfire due to a wiser-than-expected public opinion.

[I supposedly wrote additional experiences down somewhere, but they are not to be found.]

Bryan also had a vision last night. He described it in a text to me as, "…a lazy float through a brilliantly colored nebula. It was breathtakingly beautiful. I felt as if the universe was whispering to me, imparting answers to its deepest enigmas. But, that is all I could tell you it said. It was cold beyond description and while I was alone, I felt as if I were amongst millions or more. Felt in utero."

Bryan and I spoke the next day where he offered the following assessment: "It's all about understanding our taxonomic locus. We are just trapped in the middle of a hierarchy that we've just begun to explore. On one end, we look through a microscope to peer into a smaller world. On the other, another larger world peers down into ours. To say that something is inanimate is nothing short of a misnomer. Every-

Rebirth I

thing is alive in its own right and propelled by the spark of creation. If something is, it has chemical composition. There are moving parts on the atomic and subatomic levels thusly transcending everything into a machine."

February 26, 2013

While I did not have a projection, I realized the word "I" was a source of frustration in sentences.

March 2, 2013

A beautiful angel visited me this morning and told me that Bryan and I were "chosen." There is possibly an email about it somewhere between Bryan and me, but I cannot find it. We may have just talked about it on the phone.

March 3, 2013

Bryan's first daylight projection occurred today. Until this day, they have all occurred under moonlight.

March 4, 2013

The experience used the settings of a college campus, a random store, and a classroom with a professor unhappy with me because I had missed the first two days of class. The lesson was full of obstacles. I had a map that helped me find the location of the classroom. I did not believe I could walk over a suspended bridge. I finally did after people continued to pass by me, but I jumped off of the bridge and fell on my back, which resulted in me awakening from the vision. All day my fourth chakra was going crazy.

March 11, 2013

In the fragments of the vision from this morning, I could recall the word "curtsey" used as a way to show gratitude. Seven hours later at my place of employment, one of my friends managed to end a conversation by performing a "curtsey" as a gesture of the conversation's message. She had never made this gesture before, nor had anyone else in the office. We laughed about it, but I recognized the spiritual significance. Later in the evening, I spoke with Bryan. I did not share with him anything about the curtsey experience. But, in the midst of our conversation, Bryan used the word "curtsey" several times before I eventually had to ask why. He said he didn't know. He could not even recall the last time he had used that particular word. At that point, I went ahead and shared the rest of the curtsey experiences with him.

Rebirth I

March 26, 2013

This was the day of Bryan's great experience with an angel who taught him about "The Equidistant Bouquet."

April 7, 2013

Last night in my sleep, I was bestowed the opportunity to experience the primordial sound. The sound is something I have only read about – something I have imagined, but had yet to experience. My spirit was awakened from my sleep by the sound of an insect buzzing close to my face. I could not distinguish the type of insect, but rather I just became aware that a bee, a fly, or something similar was hovering over my face. As the sound of the insect intensified, so did its actions and annoyances.

The insect hovered over me and would periodically land on my face – as if to tell me to rise and awaken. Instinctively, I swatted the insect away – which seemed to be the reaction the insect wished to achieve from me. I was awake. The insect flew over to the wall where it came to rest with a swarm of other similar insects. These insects sounded like bees, but in appearance, were more like flies. The sound of the buzzing intensified. For whatever reason, my reaction to the sound and the insects was one of frustration and annoyance. I swatted the insects away. They were feisty and would not simply be scared away. I threw a pillow at the wall and fanned the area to be ridden of the insects. Eventually, they flew away and one angry wasp – red in color – flew toward me. I panicked. Scared of being stung, I threw objects at the wasp. The wasp took a beating but was intent on finding me.

The wasp eventually came to rest on my arm where I swatted it away for fear of the sting. But, the wasp never stung me. It just held on as if driven by a greater purpose. The sound of the buzzing was just as intense as ever even though the only insect I could see was the wasp resting on my arm. I ran through the house – one that I was familiar with, but unsure of where or how I had experienced this location before. Eventually I ran across a woman – a motherly figure – who seemed to know my fear and problem with the wasp before I even arrived. She took a towel and removed the wasp from my arm and in that moment, embraced me. My physical body jolted awake – my eyes opened.

My entire body was encompassed in a vibration that I have never previously experienced in any meditative state. My heart was racing. My blood was rushing through my veins. My entire state of being was in sync with a higher aetheric plane. In that moment I knew what I had experienced and I did not want to let it go. I was angry with myself for being scared – for there is nothing to fear on the spiritual plane. I longed to know more. I felt as if I had let down my Creator for not being able to understand the primordial sound I was being allowed to experience in that particular moment. All I could do was lie there – still in my bed and experience the remnants of that vibratory state.

Rebirth I

Later in the night, I was still awake but eventually became able to control the vibratory state of my body. I brought myself close to the vibratory point where I experienced the primordial sound. This reproduced experience was almost "trippy" in that the experience was disorienting and almost psychedelic with respect to the energy flows. Once I was able to channel my energy appropriately in this state and separate my mind from my body, I immediately became aware that I was standing in an empty room. My spirit was in this room asking questions into a void. I wanted to know why I was having these experiences, but nothing in greater magnitude on the earthly plane. I wanted to know why I seem so grounded on Earth, but when my spirit interacts with the ethereal plane, I cannot maintain my vibratory state. I wanted to know what God's purpose for me was. I wanted to know what I was supposed to be doing with the spiritual awareness God has given me and if God would ever directly communicate with me. And then it happened. God spoke.

I heard a voice – not an impression of a voice – but truly a voice in the void. The voice was tonally comprised of both low and high sounds. In fact, I would describe the voice as being comprised of the whole frequency spectrum – but with such a booming resonance that most would probably only notice the deepness of the sound. It was a tone that sonically could not be reproduced. God's words were simple: "This is why I have given you the ability to lucid dream." I paused when I heard His words. This was a distinct answer to the question I had just shouted out into the void and an answer to all of the ques-

The Written

tions I previously shouted out. Truthfully I saw in that moment – whether it was through my own understanding or through impressions imparted to me – that I was still a spirit child, learning the ropes of the spiritual plane.

I am still on an astral playground of sorts, waiting for my chance to play with the big kids. For me to achieve the next steps, I now know that I have to learn how to independently control my spirit, mind and body – much better than I have ever been able to achieve to date. Also, I understood that everything I can control is not due to me learning how to control it, but rather because God has given me the ability to control it. My previous thoughts were that we all have the ability within ourselves to understand the spiritual plane – which still holds true. But, the important lesson of what was impressed on me was that we may only control what is within us once God grants us the ability. Essentially, we as humans have the full potential to control and understand the spiritual realm. But, we are only given the opportunities once we have proven our worth and understanding. Nothing is controlled by our own ability. Our ability to control is gifted to us by our actions before God. And with this understanding, I found myself awake in my bed – eyes wide open – processing everything that had just occurred. I had heard the voice of God, and that was everything to me.

Rebirth I

April 13, 2013

As I watched a movie from the couch in my living room tonight, I became aware of an intriguing star outside of my window. The star was far brighter than any star I have ever witnessed from my apartment, which was the reason it drew my attention. For approximately twenty to thirty minutes I would get up from my seat, stare out the window, and try to justify the existence of this star in the sky. I searched the sky for other bright stars – which were all dimly visible in the sky.

Most of the night sky is washed out from my residence due to the city lights. I watched as helicopters flew routinely to-and-from the nearby hospitals. Still, this star remained magnitudes brighter than any other object in the sky peacefully calling for my attention. I attempted to identify the star using star charts – which, with the number of stars in the universe, I was able to justify it as being a candidate for at least one of several charted stars. Feeling content that I could justify this star as just being exceptionally bright for the evening, I returned to watching my movie.

After approximately thirty minutes from the star initially attracting my attention, this same "star" appeared in my apartment approximately two feet above the floor, and about one foot in front of a solid concrete wall. The star was approximately six feet from me and was clearly emitting its own light. The star was no bigger in size than it appeared in the distance, and I continued to have a hard time justifying that my eyes were not playing tricks on me. I sat still, soaking in the moment. I turned my head to look out the window to see the bright star from earlier. That star was no longer in the sky. I turned to look back at the "star" in my residence. My eyes were not deceiving me. As surely as every other object existed in my residence, this star was clearly there, shining extremely bright.

I stared at it for a few minutes and it slowly dissipated into the aether. I have not seen the star since that moment, but I do long for that experience again. When it returns, I will surely write about it. This experience brings so much clarity to the examples that appear in historical texts of "stars coming down from the heavens," "being visited or led by a star of light," and other such similar difficult-to-believe scenarios. Next time, I will be prepared to acknowledge the existence instead of having to justify the experience. Of such great first experiences, surely it was just a moment of acknowledgement and preparation for the next time's utmost importance and follow-through. I look forward to that day.

April 21, 2013

I found myself in a room void of anything except for a cat. This cat was an ash gray, with keen and insightful eyes. It was as if I understood everything in the void with nothing around the two of us. I began to have a conversation with the cat acknowledging my awareness of its spirit. We talked about the

Rebirth I

cat's body merely being a vessel for the spirit inside. I was having a conversation with the cat's spirit somewhat telepathically (maybe through the eyes), but there were also visual queues occurring to coincide with the conversation. During the conversation I acknowledged that I understood the spirit was the true being within the cat and that it often had to overcome biological/instinctive impulses. The cat's spirit seemed to be frustrated with that particular aspect of the situation, but had learned to cope with it (such as chasing its tail, etc.). I had the distinct impression that the spirit did not choose the body of the cat, but was making the best of the situation. The cat made a strange pawing motion into the air. It was at this point that I told the spirit of the cat that I understood the body was controlling it and that I understood the spirit had to utilize the body's vessel in the way that was biologically natural. The cat seemed pleased that I understood the line of communication we had. I came crashing out of this projection and awoke in my bed.

If anything could be taken from the projection, I would say that the conversation I had with the cat was only a microcosm to our whole existence. The spirit within our human bodies must learn how to control the body's natural tendencies and temptations. The human body has instincts that often kick in and override the spirit's ability to control it. Our goal is to allow the mind to be one with the spirit and then use the body as a vessel of existence on this Earth. Our spirit is our true essence. It is not something that just resides within us to be found and followed, but rather it is something inside of us that lies dormant until we identify it and can shift our mind away from natural human tendencies and become one with our spirit. At this point, our body is understood for what it truly is – a means of transportation and interaction within the earthly plane. We can then allow our spirit to communicate through our body. Of additional importance gleaned from the conversation with the cat is that everything living has a spirit within – thus the reason I had a conversation with a cat instead of a human entity. The spirit is at the mercy of its earthly vessel. But if you listen to it, you can learn and understand everything about it and become one with the universal consciousness.

April 22, 2013

Today, through a vision with an angelic guide, I was imparted knowledge regarding Divine Law versus Universal Law. Prior to this experience, neither of these terms existed in my mind. I came to understand that Universal Law is any law in which we as humans (and even spirits) assume to be true and just. However, the truth is that these laws can always be manipulated by our Creator. He – at His own will – can change the laws which govern our landscape. Therefore, Universal Law is not the constant that it would appear to be to the observer.

The Divine Law, on the other hand, is the law of our Father and Creator. The laws that comprise the Divine Law cannot ever be manipulated because they are core to the exist-

Rebirth I

ence of all. The first of these laws that was taught to me, was the Law of Love. This law permeates all existence in every facet. Only through our ability to Love freely and openly can we be in harmony with the Divine Law. This law may very well be the only law that underpins the Divine Law, but I do not want to classify it as such without closure from my ethereal guide. It was, however, the only law imparted to me during our interaction.

April 23, 2013
Bryan's Experience

Bryan shared with me an amazing vision from the previous night. During his sleep, his spirit left his body. He found himself immersed in an atmosphere of pink clouds. While he was soaking in the splendor of the cloudscape, a strong voice rang out in the air.

"What lies above you?" the voice asked.

Bryan answered instinctually, 'The day."

"What lies below you?" the voice asked again.

"The night," Bryan replied.

A third question came from the voice. "And in whom do you place your trust?"

Bryan replied "In the Lord, my God."

The voice was pleased as it resounded, "In this, your faith is well founded. You may now approach the East."

The Written

Bryan realized he was standing in the palm of a large hand that was holding him. This hand was all that divided the day from the night, and kept him from falling down below. Suddenly, a man appeared near the fingertips of the large hand. The man was smiling and waving for Bryan to come forward. From each of the fingertips of the large hand, rainbow light shone forth. The rainbows each followed the color order of the earthly spectrum we all became familiar with as children (**ROYGBIV**). The rainbows only extended a finite amount, but with each step the man took as Bryan followed after him, the rainbow road would extend.

The man asked, "Do you know where you are?"

It was in that moment that Bryan began to attempt to rationalize the moment. He observed everything he could and began to become aware that he felt suffocated in the moment.

He asked, "Am I breathing?"

The man replied, "You are astelic, yet I have you."

With that, Bryan became scared realizing that his earthly body was not breathing. While he understood the momentous interaction occurring in that moment, his mind and body went into survival mode as he began fearing his earthly body was dead or perhaps without oxygen and in the process of dying. Bryan came crashing back into his body gasping for breath.

He was alive, but knew that for a brief period of time, his breath had stopped in his earthly body as he was suspended in the pink clouds. He spoke to me of this story immediately this morning. It was with great excitement that he explained how he woke up gasping, but also crying tears of happiness. While

Rebirth I

he did not know who the man was that led him down the rainbow road, he felt that in some form, it must have been our Lord and Savior. Bryan went on to tell me about different events that happened to him throughout the day and during the course of his meditations. The colors all seemed brighter; the sounds so much richer. Periodically throughout the day, he experienced the voice speaking to him. It was on this day, that Bryan's life changed.

April 23, 2013
Afternoon Meditation

It should come as no surprise to me that during my reading today, the Lord would speak to me in ways to validate my previous experiences as well as Bryan's recent ethereal adventure. I decided to start reading "Heartdrops of the Dharmakaya" – one of the only western books regarding the practice of Bon from Tibet. Bon is a spirituality that Tibetans practiced to progress to a spiritual state identified as "the rainbow body." The rainbow body is said to be the final state of spiritual progression that few achieve in one lifetime, though it is possible to achieve over multiple lifetimes. There have been 180,000 documented cases of this successful metaphysical progression and the book discusses several eyewitness accounts.

In the book, it was discussed how Shardza Tashi Gyaltsen (the master and character subject of the book) practiced two kinds of bodhicitta: "one that is according to the absolute

The Written

truth, and the other according to the relative truth." The book went on to discuss the absolute and relative truths – a differentiation that would not resonate as easily with me if it were not for the vision I had a couple nights prior where the angelic guide discussed the differences of Divine Law and Universal Law with me.

These two laws were identical to the absolute and relative truths Shardza practiced in his bodhicitta! The subtleties in the way God communicates is amazing – and if you know how to understand His voice in everything around us, then it removes any doubt and questions from the oft-hard-to-rationalize interactions within the spiritual world. The book went on to discuss other intriguing points which confirmed many of the visual oddities that Bryan witnessed in his vision from the prior night.

The most striking similarity was how the Dharmakaya believe that near the final stage of spiritual completion, the body will emit light from each of the fingertips and rainbow lights will appear in the skies above. This concept basically discusses the ability to achieve on Earth the perfection that Bryan witnessed in his vision when he stood on the hand from whence rainbow light spilled forth out of the fingertips.

It should be pointed out that neither Bryan nor I had read this book, or were aware of the possibility of similarities between his vision and the Dharmakaya's philosophies. In fact, the Dharmakaya philosophies were unknown to either of us before I read the book. The only knowledge I had was that it

Rebirth I

was the only source of knowledge in English that discussed their philosophies.

Often this type of "heavenly handshake" occurs between God, Bryan, and me in a way in which we are able to confirm the content of the visions through each other's experiences in the following days and weeks.

April 23, 2013
Morning Experience

I found myself in a snowy apartment-like location. I knew I was there. The pavement was made of leaf reliefs. I thought I was going to lose it, but I did what I have read to maintain the experience. I immediately felt the ground. Everything was real....so real. I could feel it. I was chewing gum – peppermint. I thought I may lose that moment so I spun....I spun so fast I fell over but regained my balance.

I was running up a hill shouting out "God?" repeatedly. I was directed to go speak to two girls. They looked a little frustrated with me. They told me to wait just a minute. Then I heard my name being shouted. I wandered into the next room and saw a man resembling Santa Claus. I asked, "Are you God?" He said, "Hello. Who do you think I am?" I said I didn't know. He said we have met multiple times. He was a guardian.

I asked him what my purpose was. He said that he had told me the last couple of times I visited. He seemed frustrated.

I told him that I would remember now that I was in full control. I spun and I found my gravity again. He said that he was not going to keep telling me because I had not treated Arielle and the other girl well last time I was there. I was shocked. I could not believe I behaved badly. I told him it would be different – that I didn't know what it was that I was doing then and that I was completely lucid this time. He said, "That's the point. You aren't ready yet. You're not in full control." – then I found myself not there again lying on my back.

I lay there thinking I had fallen out of my projection. I was saddened and then I heard his voice. He was talking to me as if I had not left. I told him I heard him and asked him to hang on while I figured out how to return back to him. I spun and felt the ground just before I found myself back in his presence. He told me that was "truly impressive indeed" and that I had great skill. He said he has already told the others. He asked me, "What are you going to do with it?" I told him, "You better get used to it because I want to use it for good and there is no going back for me once I figure this vehicle out." He seemed extremely happy and told me, "Let's go."

I followed him to a place to pick out shoes. I thought we were going to ski, but it appeared that ice-skates were the choice du jour. He was wearing ice skates. I had to keep spinning to make sure I remained there. I picked up a pair, then thought I would demonstrate my skill of balancing my soul in this location. I tossed the shoe at my foot hoping it would magically attach to my foot. It just fell clumsily to the ground making me appear extremely childish. I tried again. It still did

Rebirth I

not work in the way I had hoped. He looked at me somewhat confused. I laughed and said, "I had to try. Is it possible that the shoes could just be tossed down and magically attach?" His look seemed disapproving like that of a child with potential who was too caught up in the magic. One of my ice-skates fell down a small slope next to where we were standing. I told him to hold on – that I would get it. Sitting down to reach the skate caused me to spin out.

    I chose to write about it to remember. Now I am back off to dreamland. Also – there was mention by one of the girls to the guy that "he needed to be ready for the group coming in." He seemed somewhat annoyed and mumbled something about "groups of people just popping in sometimes through the use of ceremonial hallucinogenics." My impression was that people trying out the technique for the first few times are not ready for the astral world and do not function well on that plane.

April 24, 2013

    Brief, in-and-out of finding a checkbook in somebody's house that it was not supposed to be in. I had a conversation about it. Nothing relevant.

April 26, 2013

During a brief encounter with "the girl" in my vision, I was told that I should not grow a beard. This puzzled me because I have only tried to grow a beard once and failed miserably in my attempt. As I stood there puzzled, she touched my cheek and while standing there I was able to perceive how she saw me with a beard.

I asked her, "Why, should I not grow a beard?"

She said, "Because you have two lines" indicating two patches on my left cheek where my facial hair did not grow.

I said, "Oh I know, that's why I wouldn't."

She seemed relieved and replied, "Good. Don't grow a beard."

I woke up shortly following this vision and initially chose to pass off the significance of my encounter. But upon discussing the dream with Bryan, he felt there was much more significance to the words said to me. Since Bryan typically finds great understanding in my visions (as I do in his), I welcomed his interpretation. He seemed very pressed to tell me to remember that not all encounters with our spiritual elders are to be taken literally – in fact, most of the time, these visions will be metaphorical to the place we are in our lives. Bryan then proceeded to tell me that he felt the words were intended to represent the internal struggle I have been facing on how to represent myself to others when negative energies attempt to re-enter my life.

Rebirth I

Bryan said the words meant that I should not let the negative energies overcome me and cause me to metaphorically grow a beard and mask my true identity. He then went on to explain the origin of the phrase "bald-face lie" which is misrepresented/misunderstood in today's culture through the use of the phrase "bold face lie." Bryan's interpretation is essentially that I need to live my life in a metaphorically clean-shaven style and to not allow who I am to be covered, altered, or otherwise masked beneath a beard. For, in that beard, my truth will still shine through and then it becomes a mixed message being broadcast to those who witness me in a metaphorical beard state.

April 27, 2013

In a lush wooded area, I became aware that I was in my spiritual body. The forest was beautiful and the colors were intoxicating. There were numerous winding streams and a large waterfall. I wandered around for some time and then decided to descend the large waterfall. The waterfall was probably two hundred feet high, if not taller. But, I was able to almost surf down the vertical incline. My feet were touching the water, but they were not dipping below the surface. Where the waterfall met the basin of the river, the water was extremely rapid. I was not scared, but I feared the current would take me further than I wanted to travel, so I stopped at the base of the waterfall and leapt off onto the damp soil on the left side of the river. I knew I was on a quest to find "the right spot" that would enable me to get closer to God.

I viewed this journey as if I was on a Sabbatical finding my spiritual center. As I began to walk up a path from the river to where I entered the woods, I became aware of a family at the entrance. As I reached the family, I saw two kids – a boy and a girl and their mother and father. I was very intrigued that another family had found the place, and for that matter, found the same entrance I had found. I knew it was significant. I asked the boy (who looked to be around eight or nine years old) if the family wanted to stay here. The parents seemed to be on a mission and the children were more or less along for the journey. The parents were getting into a vehicle and the two children were getting in the backseat. The parents shut their doors. The girl shut her door, and the boy continued to speak to me from the left passenger side with the door open. The boy continually reiterated to me that he really did want to stay here and that it was "our decision." By his response, I took it to mean that it was each of our decisions to be in the land that we were all experiencing at that moment. Curious, I asked him how they were able to consciously stay in the moment. The boy told me they were on a spiritual journey and that they drank a lot of left-handed and right-handed polarized water. The boy emphasized the words "a lot" over and over again as he told me that bit of information. It was at this point that the boy shut his door to continue on the journey with his parents and I woke up.

Rebirth I

Upon attempting to re-enter the spiritual place I was before, I found myself asking a question, "When will we…?" My question was interrupted before I was even able to finish. The bold voice from the Heavens told me, "Your answer will lie right before you." The interruption was significant because yesterday evening Bryan and I had multiple conversations where we each were struggling to understand which path to take in each of our given situations. Though each of our scenarios was different, we both decided to cut each other off due to the "manic-sounding tone" that bled through the explanation we were each attempting to convey. I knew the answer to his question before he was able to express all of the trivialities that were bogging down his sense of direction. To my frivolities and trivialities, Bryan knew the answer before I was able to finish explaining my train of thought. I believe this concept transcended to the spiritual world, because I have also been manically attempting to understand my purpose, asking God and our guardians about my purpose on Earth every chance that I am granted. Sometimes the relevance in tone would not be easily understood if it were not able to be conveyed in a manner that I could understand. By my question being cut off, I knew that God, the guardian, or whoever's voice I heard filling the void was demonstrating to me that my attempts to understand my purpose were trivial and that I just needed to listen to His word and follow the directions He placed in front of me. For therein my purpose will unfold and I can see the intention that God has for me.

May 8, 2013

Bryan's test results are in from his classes.

May 9, 2013

This morning I had a brief vision, but was unable to bring it back in words. It related to a birthday and the gift that God has been giving me. Today is my birthday, so maybe they are interrelated.

May 10, 2013

Today I woke up feeling completely different. Today is the first full day of my thirty second year on this Earth. I can't explain the feeling. The only way I can describe it is that I am new within. Everything that has happened throughout the day has echoed the command, "You are in control." God has been sharing that theme with me recently, but it is hard to understand that the world is how you shape it and intend for it to be. This could not have been reiterated to me any more clearly than at lunch.

I went into a restaurant where I ordered fish tacos. The man making my food before me looked up to ask if I wanted cheese on my tacos. I usually just say something like, "Surprise me" or "It doesn't matter. It is your choice," just to see what

Rebirth I

happens. Today was no different. I replied back with, "Your choice." The man looked at me with the austere gaze of an angel. He said, "No. You are in complete control." Those were his words. He spoke no others. Word-for-word it was just as God has been telling me. This time God's word was fed back through another on Earth. I heard God's voice telling me how I should see the world. For whatever reason, I have fallen in His graces and He has shown me so much. Perhaps it would not have been the same for me a day prior. But today – a day that I awoke feeling different – was a day that God showed me how to see the world and heaven as one.

May 8, 2013 – May 10, 2013

A summary of experiences

I am no longer who I was, yet I am everything that made me. I used to question those types of seemingly contradictory statements until the events of the last three days forever changed me. Today I am 32 years young – and in concert with my annual celebration of birth, my God has opened up a new chapter in my life. And while some may question how a new chapter in my life could coincide so closely to my birthday, to me it could not happen more noticeably in any other way. God and I have maintained a level of communication since I was a child which would manifest in the appearance of grand gestures in concert with celebrated events.

The Written

It all began when I chose to be baptized on Christmas Eve as a sign of my gift to God for the birth of His son. I could not think of a greater gesture of my faith than to formally give my life to Him on the day mankind celebrates His gift to us in the form of the birth of His son. It is true that God's divine communication to me is not limited to fancy days and moments of grand gestures, but the biggest gestures have all come in times of the greatest significance. So it came as no surprise to me – but still every bit as humbling – to witness God in motion over the course of the 3 days that surrounded my 32nd birthday.

The series of events that I am about to describe began to unfold for me on May 8th and continued through May 10th, 2013. For the better part of the prior week, my focus had been on bringing a group of people together that could collectively help carry His message forward in a manner that is focused on healing and improving the quality of life for those suffering from some of today's most challenging medical conditions. The delivery mechanism of His message is not nearly as important as the formation of the appropriate energy to deliver His message.

That energy – and those responsible for the formation of it – are of paramount importance because the collective efforts need to remain pure and un-encroached by negative intention. Through meetings and conversations with the people God continued to introduce in my life, it began to become evident that everything I once thought I understood about "divine intervention" was slowly fading into a concept more far-reaching and grandiose in design.

Rebirth I

People I had originally viewed as involved in my life for other reasons began to be spotlighted to me through God's eyes. This spotlight is difficult to explain and even much harder to recognize in experience. It would be akin to saying "I was blind, but now I see." I never was literally blind for my eyes were able to detect wavelengths and see everything around me. However, up to this point I was not able to fully interpret everything I was seeing through the eyes of the Spirit.

And again, it was not that I could not rationalize and interpret everything around me, but that any rationalization and interpretation I previously had performed was done so through my own eyes – with the ego's involvement. The distinct difference is that I realized "I" was no longer seeing the landscape around me, but my eyes were a conduit for my soul to see the landscape around me, and the spirit to interpret the meaning. Again – this is extremely difficult to explain, but at this point on May 8th, this was only the beginning of God's plan for me.

I began to realize that certain people spotlighted in my soul's eyes were all part of a divine plan that were brought into my life for His purpose. This was not my personal will or intention. Rather, it was God's will and intention speaking through me. I was merely observant – listening to His will – and most importantly, responding to His directions. His purpose of bringing these people together is far greater than just a name, a label, a business concept, or delivery construct could express. It is far greater than the ideas I can verbally express in order to bring them together – and in that, there is recognition deep within each of our souls that we are following His intended direction.

May 11, 2013

Bryan had a vision relating to my vision on the 9th. He was told, "A breeze stirs; invite him to approach; slice it through; polish your spirit with the Love of God (Kami)."

May 12, 2013

My experience began in a setting similar to my apartment in Nashville. A group of three girls walked in the front door. Everyone wanted to talk to me. They were not flirty, but they were socially flirty – as if I was someone they recognized and wanted to be around. This carried on for a bit as we all sat on the couch and chairs in the living room. I decided to change clothes and walked back to the closet in my bedroom. When I returned, the couch was missing from my apartment. I struggled for a moment trying to figure out how my couch just up and vanished in those few minutes. It took me longer than it should have for the reality to sink in. Once I had it all sorted out in my mind, one of the three girls wrote each of their names on my coffee table where only I could see. All three names began with the letter A. The first name was "Afelicia" (or something similar to it). The second name was "Ana___" (I think the remainder was "stacia" but I could not read it well).

Rebirth I

The third name began with an A as well, but I was unable to recall the name in my journal. All three were brunette and very beautiful.

A motherly angel appeared in my room. I confirmed with her that I was indeed missing my couch and that I was in control of my soul in that moment. She confirmed and we transitioned into a hallway. A young girl around the age of five appeared. I was instructed to protect her at all costs. We ran down the hallway as an older obese man chased us. When he cornered us at the end of the hallway, I gave him a quick one-two punch to the face and then the gut. I surprisingly knocked him down. I shouted something along the lines of, "My God is my strength and you will not defeat me with Him at my back."

The man stood up and smiled at me as if I had passed the test. He exited through a door to my right. I then went into a library where five to seven assailants attacked us. I put the girl behind a large desk and grabbed a handful of pencils. They were the only sharp objects I could find. The little girl began tapping on my back with one of the pencils. At that moment, I lunged toward the first attacker and stabbed him in the heart with the pencil. He fell down. I was in shock. I could not tell if he was dead or not. The other attackers were unsure how to proceed because they knew they would lose. I have never killed anyone and I did not like being in that situation. Unfortunately, I knew that the only way I could truly protect the girl was to make sure the assailants were killed or incapacitated as they approached me. There was no other option. It was uncomfortable and I did not like it. The world began to spin and

I kept shouting out to anyone listening that "I was in control" of my harmony in this experience. Unfortunately I could not hold on and I awoke.

May 24, 2013

On my way back from Chattanooga with my daughter, we passed by a campsite on the edge of a lake. I told her that we should count how many people were camping out for Memorial Day weekend. I was pretty confident that I had never mentioned the word "camping" around her before, and it was an abnormal subject to bring up with her. But, since I have recently felt a calling to take an extended backpacking adventure, I thought I would bring the subject up to her. She immediately became very excited and told me how badly she has been wanting to go camping recently. She is only seven years old, so naturally I asked her what prompted her to want to go camping. All she could explain to me was that over the last few weeks she has felt a strong feeling that she should go camping.

She is acutely aware of her subconscious, but unable to put into words precisely how she recognizes the feelings. I asked if her mom, kids at school, a television show, or anything influenced her decision. She said no – and that she really had no idea why it was on her mind. What she did not know was that over the last few weeks, I had had a strong urge to take a backpacking sabbatical also. I had not camped or backpacked

Rebirth I

ever in my life, so it had been an unusual desire for me. But, in answering the calling, I had focused all of my spare time over the last few weeks on choosing the right backpacking gear and ordering everything I needed. No one aside from one friend had any idea that I was experiencing this call into the wilderness.

Everything my daughter was feeling was undeniably tied to the feelings I was having. While there have been other occurrences of shared thought with her, I wanted to make sure I wrote this one down. Two people, separated in age by twenty-five years, by distance of two states, and in six hours of drive time, were sharing the same unusual thoughts of going into the wilderness.

May 25, 2013
Early Morning

After closing my eyes, I immediately came to the realization that I was standing in a store – possibly a bank. The person standing before me handed me a stack of cash. The person did not have an identity that I could recognize – he was represented by a dark colored form with no face. It seemed as if the money was either change or payment for something I had already given him. The cash was not neatly stacked, so I quickly sorted through the bills to make the stack a little neater while I discreetly checked to see if I was handed the right

The Written

amount (though I couldn't tell you what the amount was supposed to be).

One of the bills seemed unusual. While all of the other bills appeared to be of U.S. currency, one bill (that in a quick glance, I initially thought to be a $5 bill) had a yellowish color to it. It was clearly different than all of the other bills. While I recognized it was unusual, I did not want to draw attention to the fact I was double-checking the stack of cash given to me. I quickly folded the bills and stuffed them into my pocket. A few seconds passed when I decided to inspect the different bill again. This time as I unfolded the stack, the bill appeared to be a $10 denomination from the backside. The bill had a scene on it that I rationalized as being a commemorative design – similar to how the USA has commemorative quarters unique for each state. This particular bill had a scene with a modernized cowboy on it as well as Abraham Lincoln (hence why I thought a $5 bill in the beginning). The two individuals were talking about the south.

As I finished inspecting the bill, I was immediately transported to a room where I was staring at a wall where the word "Wellington" appeared in a western-Elizabethan styled font. I sensed the importance of the moment, so I recited the word in my head. I then saw flashes of the word "Washington" in place of "Wellington." I recited "Lincoln-Washington-Wellington" over and over again because I knew that I was being imparted an important piece of knowledge. Though I could not discern what the words meant in that particular moment, it was the second time I had a vision involving the

Rebirth I

yellowish-colored commemorative $10 bill placed into a stack of money handed to me. In the previous vision, I had failed to recall the details with confidence so I did not document the vision. This time I knew the most important thing to do was to remember in vivid detail the content of the vision, write it down immediately and speak to Bryan about his interpretation. Of all of the visions I have had, this one was the most confusing to date. I was unsure if Wellington was a name or a city and if there was any significance to the yellowish-colored currency.

After researching the word "Wellington," I discovered it was the capital of New Zealand and a coveted location for extended backpacking trips. I subsequently found out that the New Zealand $5 bill was very close to the design and color of the unusual $5/$10 bill in my vision. Again, I had never seen any New Zealand currency and had never had an interest in the country. A quick search for "Wellington, Washington, and Lincoln" yielded results that told the tale of Wellington, Washington – a small town reachable only by backpacking and was the site of a disastrous avalanche in 1910 killing 95 people. My recent desire to backpack into the wilderness made both discoveries intriguing, but the latter slightly more interesting to me – for in the last few weeks, I had been purchasing all of the supplies needed to backpack in the wilderness for an extended period. However, I could find nothing in the research of my vision that was clear, so I deferred to Bryan for his interpretation.

The Written

In what is becoming a regular occurrence, Bryan was able to offer a divine interpretation to the vision. Bryan brought forth that the vision was not to be taken literally. Instead, the actions of the vision's events held the answer to the meaning. He explained that the currency being handed to me was extremely important on several levels. The first level of importance was the symbolic nature of the transaction. I was given cash that included a unique piece of currency. This unique currency was the clue that the cash was to be understood as something greater than spending power – it was something that transcended the literal. The cash represented knowledge and the experiences I have received from our spiritual elders. The unusual-colored piece of currency was the clue that I had been given something special. Bryan went on to tell me that it is of utmost importance to understand that the knowledge I had received along my spiritual journey is not to be not be treated as commonplace and should not be used ("spent") in the same way that other knowledge would typically be used ("spent"). The knowledge I have received (and have yet to receive) has a greater purpose. Much like money should be treated as a tool to help facilitate the spreading of this knowledge – and not be used for personal gain – the cash represented the value of the knowledge and experiences I have received.

The second part of my vision was to be recognized as an attempt at communication regarding the strong feelings I had been having regarding backpacking in the wilderness. Wellington and the currency design were keys that caused me to

Rebirth I

recognize the common theme of backpacking – escaping from the hustle and bustle of modern life. The purpose of the word "Wellington" was to bring my spirit into recognition of its central desire and truth. Bryan went on to explain that the strong desire I have to find solitude in the wilderness is my physical answer to a spiritual desire. My spirit had been pushing me – calling out to me to cross into new territory that requires extreme discipline and discovery. Much in the way that many of our revered elders achieved spiritual enlightenment during sabbaticals and fasting in the desert, long periods of wandering in nature, and extreme periods of solitude – their journeys were physical answers to spiritual desires. For in our lives, a spiritual action cannot occur without a physical counterpart – and likewise in return, the physical action will always represent the spiritual intention. And while people may act out a physical action that is representative of an intention they hope to feel spiritually, the action will not carry the same meaning if the desire is not first charged by the spirit.

So in my quest for answers and understanding of what I was supposed to do and where I was supposed to travel, I missed the crucial intersect that the words and symbols in my vision were just tools to help me recognize the spiritual desire inside of me – the money changing hands representing the extreme value that the knowledge holds, and the care I should take in determining how to distribute all that I have and will eventually learn. We asked questions while seeking answers through how someone else may have answered a similar desire or vision. We often rely on other people's experiences to form our own answers to the questions posed. The problem is that the questions were never questions to begin with. The answers we sought were actually just the recognitions of the knowledge being imparted – and the growth in learning how to listen. Listening is all that is required. Fully divested of ego, our physical body will enact the spiritual desire when it is heard – the physical mirror of its spiritual intention.

Bryan and I discussed the depth of the experience and how it was deeper than surface level indicated and that we should be cognizant in listening to our spirit. In closing, he shared with me these inspired words: "The benefit of someone else's experience is a guidepost, not an answer." His quote can be echoed in all avenues of our lives, and I am still finding new significance in its very meaning when applied to every question to which I seek an answer.

May 25, 2013
Update pertaining to previous experience

Just an update found in news today. Apparently a slow-motion 7.0 earthquake has been dragging on for five months under New Zealand.

Rebirth I

May 25, 2013
Evening phone call with Bryan

Bryan had an AP of opening holes in the aether and passing through them repeatedly.

May 31, 2013

Last night I was surrounded by Bryan, a female that had a strong bond to him, and another couple (guy and girl). We were getting off a plane in what appeared to be India – or someplace of similar culture. We went to the hotel, which turned out to be more like a single-level house with no doors on the inside. It exhibited a completely open floor plan. As Bryan and the girl he was with began to unload their bags, I was asked to go along with the other couple. I thought we were going to the beach, but could not be entirely be sure.

We proceeded to a destination in a Jeep-like vehicle and parked after finding the very best parking spot (up front next to the entrance of the beach access point). As we were parking, someone pulled in behind us and seemed frustrated that there were no more parking spots in the entire lot for them, so they left. The parking lot was made of sand. We had music playing very loudly just enjoying the moment.

When we got out of the Jeep, we decided to keep the music playing since it was loud enough to hear at the beach. The couple ran in through the gate in front of me. I realized that we did not have cell phones and had not stopped to buy a disposable phone once we landed, so I was concerned that Bryan would not know where we went. I was frustrated about not having communication, but decided the point of this trip was to not have any technology interfere with the events. I proceeded to go through the main entrance toward the beach. I was suddenly in a room where everyone was worshiping in silence. The sound of the music playing from the vehicle was so loud, it could be heard inside. I found the couple and they looked embarrassed, as was I. In the moment though, we laughed and I decided to slide out the way we had arrived. I decided to walk back to the hotel.

During my walk, I saw the couple drive by me in the Jeep-like vehicle. Eventually, I made it back to the hotel where Bryan still was. We discussed communication and how we should go about making sure we knew where everyone was. Again, it was still decided that technology needed to be removed from the equation – no cell phones, etc. – even though we feared becoming lost from one another and the others in the group.

June 1, 2013

Tonight I knelt before the Lord, my God. I began to speak out loud about the joy, Love and awe I had begun to feel over the last several days. The only way I could think to describe the feelings welling up within me over the last several days would be to say it was like falling in Love – so deeply that

Rebirth I

you want to tell everyone about it, knowing all along that there is no possible way anyone could grasp the intensity of your feelings in those moments. It is like a helpless feeling of amazing happiness, joy, and Love all bursting out from deep inside with no one there to experience the feeling with you.

As the first words to my prayer began to form on my lips, I realized that my conversations and prayers with God would forever be changed. He, our all knowing Creator – aware of all that was, and all potentialities of what will become – constantly reaches out and speaks to us in ways that have fallen on blind eyes and deaf ears. It was not that I did not observe the world around me, nature, the actions and words of others. It was not that I did not recognize when I was being guided – gently nudged in His intended direction for me. It was that this particular form of communication did not communicate to me on a level deeper than instinctual. It was as if I was now becoming fluent in a language that I had been translating and understanding throughout all of these years. And in this moment, I knew that I could never communicate with God in the same way again.

For me to ask of Him anything would be the same as me telling Him that I still do not "get it" and never will. For me to ask a question, means I do not know how to listen, know how to hear his words, nor know how to speak with Him. Truly there is no question I have that requires an answer for me to continue on my journey. And, there is no situation I am in that He does not already know about that I could ask for help or guidance. His hand is constantly guiding my journey – gently nudging me toward the destination. But it falls upon my shoulders to hear the voice of God, see His hand, acknowledge His presence, and continue forward. There is no reverse. There is only one finish line, and it remains ahead of me.

Now that I am aware of this level of communication, to ignore it or revert back to the way I previously communed with God would be no different than me telling Him directly that I do not accept this next step in my spiritual growth. By no stretch of the imagination is this acceptable. Perhaps someone who has not yet spoken to God, or been in the presence of His angels would have more proverbial slack in their spiritual line per se, but for me, I am now held to a higher standard – a standard that I have accepted to be the next baseline on my spiritual journey.

So, as I sat there, puzzled about what to say to God – I decided to tell Him just that. I told Him that for the first time in my life I had no idea what to say. I had no more questions because I now understood that I already have all of the answers – and when I perceive to need help, I know He is already responding. I told Him that it was awe-inspiring and humbling, and that I would ask only for His patience with me. I always strive to be quick and fluid in my growth and understanding, but this level is entirely new for me and so I acknowledged that a stumble and a fall – despite however frustrating it may be for me in my growth – is still a step forward. I closed with asking for strength in allowing me to always maintain my eyes of wonder – to see the world through a child's

Rebirth I

eyes – keen and drawn to all of the magic and intrigue in the mysteries of life.

In that moment, it became as if I was standing on the cusp of a grand new landscape overlaying the world in which I currently live. That landscape has yet to be traversed by me, but from this point on, I have no option but to rise to the occasion. Anything less would be painting a picture of a destiny that I did not desire. As I pondered all of these thoughts, I came to the realization that there is only one real question I have about anything – and the answer has no impact on my life, and has zero impact on my destination. The answer only serves to fill a mild curiosity I have – but one that I recognize I already know the answer deep within my soul. That question: is this the first generation of my soul as a human on Earth, or is this another version of me? I like to believe that I would risk it all – the possibility of not remembering my true identity and place among the Heavens – to come back to this Earth and help teach others and learn from others about the Love of God and our purpose.

On more than one occasion I have begged God to tell me my purpose. It seemed to be the greatest mystery of my existence. But just as strongly as I felt I had no answer, I now know the answer has been around me all along. Our purpose is all the same. We are each lenses of our Creator. Everyone is a part of God. To look at someone and see them as distinct is a false understanding of what a person is, for we are not a "who," we are a "what." And to understand that we are all lenses of the same Almighty Love will change a mindset forever.

June 1, 2013

Bryan called me today to tell me about his experience from the prior evening. He was taken to a room with stark white walls and a red floor. The room was minimalist in nature. There were two people who entered the room who were very familiar to him. They walked over to him. It was at this moment, that Bryan realized he was standing in a funeral parlor – and that the parlor represented his residence. One of the men addressed Bryan.

"Do you know what happened?" he asked. Bryan acknowledged that he did. The man then instructed Bryan to go clean out his closet. Bryan went into the adjoining room and began to sort through the drawers of the dresser. In the top drawer, everything was pink in color. It was at this point that he realized that all of the items in the drawer represented memories. The term "precipitous memories" came to mind. He knew this was an important moment. From this point forward, he could not allow any memories to drive his life.

Bryan returned to the main funeral parlor – this time no one was there. The room's design had changed slightly. The walls, the floor – any material structure in the instant all looked like a scene from an oil painting. Everything had a slight shimmer and fluid appearance to it.

Rebirth I

As Bryan was soaking in the mesmerizing visuals of the room, a female angel appeared in the room. With no lips moving, but with the crystal-clear sound of a voice, she said to Bryan, "You have done everything you need to do here. Don't you think it would be better if Jonathan was here?"

Bryan stood speechless. He replied with a simple, "How?"

She said, "Call to him."

With that, Bryan ran out the door in the room as if he instinctively knew what to do. Outside the door it was just him and the darkness. There was a sky above and a sky below. Bryan was running between the two skies on the horizon where the two skies met. With each step the skies appeared to pull away from him. He also felt a splashing beneath his feet.

Bryan called out my name, "Jonathan!!! You've gotta come here!!!" His voice was distorted, somewhat akin to the oily visualizations he had just witnessed. The oily concept had transcended into his voice.

Nearly instantly, I replied back, "Where are you?"

Bryan replied, "I'm everywhere and nowhere at once." And in that moment, I appeared before him. The skies quit pulling away from each other. I appeared before him (in his words) as a "wild-eyed child full of wonder – like I had just seen Santa Claus."

I looked at Bryan and asked, "Where is here?"

His response was simple. "I don't have answers for everything. I came out of the building behind me."

I appeared confused, for there was no building behind Bryan. I asked him what building he was talking about, and

The Written

what the building was. Bryan could only pull together the words, "That building was my mind. I don't know what to call it."

Curious, I said, "Let's find out more!!!" and we began running into the infinite skies behind him. As we were running, the elevation of the terrain never changed, but there became a sensation of running up a hill. I was running to Bryan's right. As we ran, on the left side of Bryan, a manifestation of God incarnate appeared. He was translucent in form with white defined edges and had a glimmer/glow surrounding Him. The appearance would probably more aptly be described as a representation of God in human form, but nevertheless, He appeared before us. God was leaning against an empty shelf. It was as if God wanted to let us know that He was there, witnessing our progress. Old memories were no longer required to move forward. The empty shelf was symbolic for the world of possibilities that lie ahead. Then God impressed these words to Bryan: "Now everything is up to you to write the next chapter." The manifestation of God incarnate faded away.

From here, I disappeared into the aether as quickly as I had arrived and Bryan found himself back in his bedroom. He touched the clock by his hand as if to verify he was back on Earth. As his hand made contact with the clock, he heard an angel speak one parting set of words to him: "This is your time."

Prior to this vision, Bryan had no idea I had just prayed for help in maintaining my eyes of wonder. Yet his description

Rebirth I

of when I appeared in front of him included the reference – and my personal metaphor from the movie, "Rise of the Guardians." This was a seven-and-seven moment.

June 4, 2013

I found myself standing in a void. In front of me stood a male angel. To his left was a female. She was stark and beautiful – naturally so. She was not the kind of natural beauty that we find here on Earth such as those who have long lashes, large eyes, and beautifully-flowing hair. She was much simpler. She stood tall, svelte, and thin with a milky white complexion. Her lips were a rosy red, which stood out in contrast to her complexion. Her eyes were smaller and colored a steel gray that radiated happiness and wonder. The shape of her eyes was like a morning sunrise cresting over the horizon, a type of eye I like to call "sunshine eyes" due to the feelings they invoke in me. One look into her eyes and I could find myself lost in eternity. Her hair was light blonde (not platinum and not white or silver). The color was one not known to us here on Earth. Her hair was styled straight and plain, but somehow perfect in every way. Her features were simple, plain, and unpronounced. An elegant, but simple baby-blue dress fell across her thin frame. I believe in all of her simplicity I found a beauty unknown to me until that very moment.

I became aware of a crowd surrounding us mixed in gender and race. As I was being pulled deeper into the moment,

The Written

soaking in every detail that I could, the girl suddenly fell lifelessly to the floor. With a booming voice, the angel standing to her right proclaimed aloud, "Does anyone know CPR?"

I stood there, speechless. For just a fraction of a second, I surveyed the crowd. Everyone appeared unsure of how to help or was either too scared to try. One man in particular, muttered under his breath that he did know CPR but could not help. He appeared frightened and scared that he may fail.

Almost instantly I cried out "I do!" as I ran to her side. She was lying lifelessly on her left side – her head to my right as I faced her. I touched her body. Cold. Lifeless. I drew my hand to her neck to check for a pulse. I could not find one. I rolled her onto her back and began to perform chest compressions.

Somehow in this moment I had the feeling she had drowned – as if she had actually just been pulled from a body of water and not collapsed before me. As I ended the first set of compressions, I placed my first finger and thumb to her chin to tilt her head for mouth-to-mouth resuscitation. Her head was light; her jaw was soft but somehow distinctly defined as it rested with a slight tilt against my hand. I leaned in and our lips touched as I began to breathe. While she exhibited no movement, it felt as if she coyly attempted to reciprocate my gesture with a small kiss during that moment. While I knew no one could notice that subtle movement of her lips, I remained thoroughly confused as to how this all could happen. I thought that it had to be involuntary muscle spasms. I desperately tried to rationalize what seemed so clearly to be a kiss.

Rebirth I

I continued alternating compressions and mouth-to-mouth resuscitation. Each time our lips would touch, there was a more pronounced effort by her to kiss. The third time it became so obvious that as my lips surrounded hers while breathing air into her mouth – I feared others would start to notice her lips moving. However, all I could focus on in that moment was making sure she was alive. She was not breathing, but somehow strangely able to kiss. Surely this was my mind playing tricks on me. I remained strong in my effort to revive her though I began to desire a real kiss from her.

As our lips parted the third time, she rolled onto her left side, spit out some water and took in a big breath of air. She lay there smiling – almost playfully with eyes full of joy. Her eyes were fixed onto mine. She sat up and we found ourselves face-to-face. While I had never met her before, I felt that I already knew everything about her. The only way I could describe the feeling is how someone may come to know a lot about a celebrity (movie star, musician, etc.) without having ever met them previously. My heart was racing. I could tell her heart was racing too. She leaned in to kiss me. As our lips touched and began to part open wider, I backed off. I looked at her and told her that it felt wrong and confusing. I had just saved her life, yet now she wanted to kiss. I wanted to, but there were so many mixed emotions as to what was actually occurring. We stared deep into each other's eyes – getting more deeply lost in the other with each passing second. All of a sudden, with no words spoken, she said everything and nothing at once to me.

The Written

In that moment I came to understand infinity and unconditional Love. I did everything I could to save her life. I showed unconditional Love toward her in such a way that I put aside conventions, fears and distractions and focused only on bringing her back to life. And as I breathed each breath – the very essence of life into her mouth and lungs, she attempted to reciprocate my effort by showing her returned Love to me through the kisses. Her attempts to kiss me while I tried to revive her were indeed real. While confusing, they were not just in my mind. It was such a clear demonstration of the circular bond of Love that upon this realization, I could only stare back into her eyes as if to say, "I understand. You saw me. And, now, I see you."

Glassy eyed, she leaned in to kiss again – this time I exhaled all of my reservations and leaned in to meet her in the middle. Our lips touched – soft, slightly parted – the kiss electrified every part of my soul. In that kiss, I came to understand true Love. This was not puppy Love, sexual, sensual, parental, family, marital, passion, or any other Love I had ever experienced. This was the Love at the heart of Love – Love's true center. The feeling was overwhelming and all encompassing to my very being. It permeated my soul like light trapped inside of a container, bursting to get out. And as we kissed, the male angel beside her nodded and I found myself back on Earth.

I believe that she was never really drowning or in danger. I believe it was just another lesson or a test given to me by the angel that never left her side. He stood there stoic and proud both during her collapse and after – clearly in the role of the

Rebirth I

instructor to me on my journey. He introduced the test/lesson to me so that I might demonstrate my progress to date as well as experience another lesson in understanding the Divine Law (the law of Love). It is one thing to read, become knowledgeable and understand, but it is an entirely different understanding to experience it. I believe the remarkable feeling I felt trumps any other feeling I have ever experienced in my life. Simple. Blissful. Full. Warm. I was whisked away on the very essence found at the core of the earthly experience we call "Love" – the fundamental reason for our purpose and existence. Words will never be able to describe how much that moment was filled with divine knowledge and spiritual awareness. The best hope to illustrate the feeling is for every experience a person has on Earth regarding Love, envision a feeling infinitely more perfect in every aspect. It is only then that a person can begin to conceive the feeling of the circular, infinite, unconditional Love of the heavens.

June 11, 2013

Last night I appeared in the void. In front of me, was a large desk. A woman casually sat behind it looking at me with eyes full of intrigue. The only word I could adequately use to describe her was "Lovely." And while the word "Lovely" may have its roots and peak usage from a time period that reaches further back than a century ago, I can now imagine how it must have felt when that word was first uttered into existence

The Written

to describe such a person with similar qualities to the woman sitting before me. It always intrigues my mind when one word can portray someone so exquisitely and precisely, a word exhibiting such a unique medley of traits wherein the definition of the traits themselves actually pale in comparison to the overall impact of the word that they comprise – which in this case, consist of warmth, joy, and Love.

The woman rose to her feet and proceeded to walk over to me. But perhaps "walk" is not the appropriate word– "walking on air, or gliding" may more adequately describe the fluidity and ease of her movements. As she moved toward me, her face was flushed in joy even though she appeared to attempt to curtail the amount of joy I could perceive.

While I did not know the woman, I felt as if I already knew everything about her – her history. She had a familiarity that has become such a consistently recurring feeling in this new world I am being allowed to experience. It was in these first moments of seeing her that I became aware of her role as "the receptionist." In essence, she was an angel – my guide – the spiritual visage that was there to meet me upon my arrival.

We spoke for a few minutes, making small talk about her past. It was in the presentation of her role and the familiarity which I experienced in the conversation with her that I began to confuse her with another person I know on Earth. While I understand the confusion I was experiencing was merely my mind rationalizing and trying to make sense of my surroundings, the confusion began to distort the reality of the moment.

Rebirth I

As our conversation progressed, I became entrenched in a mental war with myself regarding the angel's identity.

For a moment, imagine standing next to your closest friend, talking about their past, their present, their future; laughing and conversing as if you had known each other forever. The feeling that permeates the soul and describes that particular moment in time – the recognition of knowing another on such a deep level – is so distinct, so clear. It is unmistakable. Now imagine all of those feelings rushing inside of your very being while suddenly not being able to visually distinguish who the person is and not remembering the person's name, or anything else about them. It is a feeling of knowing everything and not knowing how or why you know everything all at once. This is the feeling that has been recurring to me in each of these experiences.

To be honest, this is the cause/effect that distorts many of the experiences in the heavens we are blessed to have. This distortion leads to confusion for many. The mind is a powerful thing. The brain subconsciously detects patterns, shapes and faces all while rationalizing familiarities. It is why we see shapes in the clouds and faces in terrain photos. In my particular experience at this time, if my mind did not fight reality versus rational understanding, the experience would have quite possibly never existed. The experience is similar to how one cannot look directly into the face of God. The experience would be too overpowering for the mind to process. It, more or less, creates a spiritual overload. "My cup runneth over" takes on a whole new meaning. Much in a similar manner to

The Written

the previous example, our experiences in the heavens with the angels are so tremendously overpowering that the brain must rationalize the moment in order to sustain the experience. Without the rationalization, the experience would be incomprehensible and therefore would not ever exist.

So, returning to the moment in the heavens for me, "the receptionist" and I continued to talk, but the conversation began morphing into a conversation I would normally have with the similar earthly person. Every time I began to merge the heavenly and earthly realities in conversation, I struggled to form sentences. Yet, she remained unphased. I believe the struggles I was having actually caused her to become more enraptured in the moment. I felt an increasing amount of warmth and Love from her the longer we talked.

She eventually began to exude a Love toward me amidst the conversation that was somewhere between the definitions of passion and intimacy. She told me she knew I was lonely, but said so in a way that was full of warmth and full of genuine care. (And the truth is I have not been in a relationship for quite some time – but that has been a voluntary decision during my quest for greater personal and spiritual growth.) The angel continued to tell me that Love was important and that she wanted to help me. She did so in a way that resonated with my limited understanding of the lesson of "universal Love" from my last lesson in the heavens. Ensuring I felt Loved seemed to be of utmost importance to her. She pushed me backwards into a small room (a closet perhaps) and began to embrace me. The words she kept pleading for me to remember while repeating over and over to me were, "Let me take care of it. I can take care of it." The intention in her words was not to portray sexuality, but rather to express her desire to help my soul experience universal Love. She felt my pain – found the hole in my soul – and wanted to help me feel completion.

My mind was reeling. I already was fighting a mental battle of her identity, though I truly knew she was an angel and not the earthly friend. My conscience struggled with the moment – overloading at the thought of what was about to happen. My rational mind continued to remind me of my earthly friend's fiancé. Indeed, she was engaged to be married and I would never cross any line that would damage that Love for her. That feeling grew stronger within me, but whether I believed it or not, I knew that my conscience was the answer to the situation.

I pushed my way out of the angel's light embrace. While nothing physical had yet happened – and I wasn't even sure if something would occur – all signs pointed in that direction. I opened the door and stepped away from her in the direction of the door. I told her that I was sorry, but I could not in good conscience continue forward since she was engaged. I knew the angel wasn't engaged, but I also knew that my mind rationalizing the moment of her as my earthly friend, meant that my true essence would be exposed with whatever decision I was to make. For if the experience was to occur with any doubt of the reality of the experience, then my essence would reflect negatively. I would rather accept a delay on experiencing universal Love and instead show that due to my mind's rationale, I would rather abstain from doing anything that contradicted the essence of my conscience.

The angel's facial reaction told me everything. She had a brief look of confusion that quickly transitioned to a look of understanding for my decision. But, that look fleeted quickly. Her face became filled with hope, with pride, with wonder that gave me confidence in my decision. But in all of those emotions I sensed her core to be laced with an empathic sadness that I could only understand to be due to her not yet being able to fill the hole in my soul with the experience of universal Love that she was clearly capable of providing to me. There was no emotion driven by ego – only Love. Universal Love. Unconditional Love. And in that moment, I knew there would be another – and in that other, a cosmic healing and understanding of universal Love. Until that day, I can only patiently wait in exalted anticipation.

June 11, 2013

The voice of the spirit spoke through me today. As I pondered religions, the necessities of steps required for people to understand God, each person's divine purpose here on Earth, and the personal journeys on which we must embark – I became charged at the idea of ministering to others and helping them grow spiritually with the all of the knowledge that has been shared with me. I pondered the names of each main-

Rebirth I

stream religion, their revered leaders, the names of the churches and synagogues they attend. I became aware that the spiritual understanding I had gained could not be aptly described with one word since it really is the understanding of everything that is, and everything that isn't. I silently searched for a word in the depths of my mind that could describe the essence of God. Nearly instinctively, I blurted the word "Teja" aloud. For just a millisecond, I saw the word appear in my head. And, as suddenly as it appeared, the pronunciation rolled across my lips (tay-yah).

Having never heard or seen the word before, nor having any idea why the word came dashing across my lips, I decided to look up the meaning of the word. As it turns out, "teja" is a word from a ten-thousand-year-old language – Sanskrit. The Sanskrit definition of "teja" means "radiance." I could not think of a more appropriate word to describe the concept I was attempting to define: the "essence of the Spirit." Words are meant to evoke a specific combination of thoughts and feelings in people. They are carefully chosen to relay a specific significance. This word, which I now know was spoken through me by the Spirit, is of utmost importance in describing the very essence of all we are trying to achieve. Mankind, through personal spiritual journeys, is on a quest to seek out and achieve teja – not just for themselves, but for others.

Even more significance can be placed on the word, teja, when it is translated into ancient Hebrew (the basis of all spoken languages). Much like the Hebrew word for God (YHWH – pronounced Yah-way) is composed of 4 letters and two syllables, the word teja (THYH or TAYH depending on how it would actually have been spelled) contains the same linguistic construct. The word YHWH is comprised of the letters Yod Hey Vav Hey. In Hebrew, each letter in a word carries multiple meanings. Unlike in English where we say "the letter A is for Apple," in Hebrew each letter actually has a distinct definition and associated numeric value (since there were no number characters in the alphabet, the first letter of the alphabet would represent the number one and so on.). The first letter of each word indicates the relationship of the definition of the word to the cardinal meaning of the first letter – meaning, the first letter of a word will most closely relate to the words overall definition. By letter definition, the word YHWH means "The right hand of revelation, brings the nail of revelation." To put our new word into perspective, the word teja (THYH) would mean "The divine revelation of the right hand of revelation." In the alternative spelling of teja, TAYH would mean "The divine strength of the right hand of revelation." In either case, clearly the word teja has an extremely strong relationship to the word meaning "God" in Hebrew. I personally feel that even by Hebrew definition, the word Teja could best be thought to describe the "essence of God." With the understanding of the Hebrew meaning, the Sanskrit translation of "radiance" carries even greater significance than before.

Today I was undoubtedly imparted a divine word for the religious concept I was seeking to define and further understand. I had never read Sanskrit, nor ever heard of the word "teja" until today. Through research, I came to learn the

Rebirth I

word's origin and meaning could not be just be coincidence – instead, this could only further add affirmation to the divine influence that flowed through me today. From this point forward, I think it is prudent to use the word "teja" to mean the "Radiance/Essence of God." By definition, the word should mean this: that which we hope to seek out and discover on our spiritual journeys, but also in others. Teja is what we should all be striving to achieve.

June 13, 2013

Bryan and I discussed the greyhound analogy the previous night. If all we had was one life, then good enough may be all that matters. BUT IF there is more to the greater picture, then good enough is the equivalent of failing. Bryan talked about me wanting to try hard because if we have one shot, we cannot rest on our laurels. We should always be listening. Remaining calm should be status quo. Greatness should be what we strive for. The message is one of Hope and how we should aspire for greatness even if we do not know how to make the next move.

Today at work I took notice as my boss, Alex, took extra time to show care about a candidate's intention in his job search rather than just treating him as another resume to get placed. This was a little unusual since our company generally demands high volume and low interaction. That is why I took notice. It was different this time and a message that God wanted me to witness.. The candidate he spoke to felt misplaced in his current job. A little while after I took notice of the conversation, Alex pulled me aside to discuss how to help me get "where I need to be." It was not a conversation about changing jobs – and actually, in context, it was rather spiritual even if that was not his intention. Rather, it was to help me achieve more than I had been able to accomplish so far. Internal opportunities were discussed that could help me continue moving upward. The important point was that he noticed I was misplaced and wanted to help me move in the direction I needed to go. He was the catalyst of the conversation I spoke about earlier.

June 15, 2013

Bryan awoke saying "Nath" which is a Sanskrit term for "Lord, protector, refuge." He was unaware what the word meant until we searched for its meaning in Sanskrit while we spoke. When he was shared the word, he was encompassed in a body of rainbow light. We talked about the physical embodiment of the spirit's direction such as wind on the face and dancing. Those concepts made me recall the previous years after turning 30 and not seeing a pinhole of light. Bryan and I discussed different points in our past that made us recognize the eerie familiarity with each other.

Rebirth I

June 16, 2013

The following is the transcript of a conversation Bryan had with God in the heavens. The conversation occurred twice in a row:

Bryan: Amidst a rainbowed maelstrom, the discourse began:

"Where am I?" – Bryan

"In flux." – God

"What am I?" – Bryan

"The sum of your choices, not of your mistakes." – God

"So, I am?" – Bryan

"Yes, you Are!" – God

"All systems are go! Light up, or lights out! Pensée du Jour: Even a nanosecond can encamp an eternity." – This was a message from Bryan to me at the bottom of the transcript.

Very few times will I ever say that the subject I am about to discuss crosses the boundaries of the capacity of the human mind. But, in the following moments it will become evident that the spiritual experiences that took place over the three day period surrounding June 15, 2013, cross the comfort level boundary that most people would have regarding this particular subject matter.

The recent eighteen months have been a whirlwind of spiritual growth, understanding, and heavenly experiences that defy and breach the barriers that each and every religion around the globe sets out to establish. However, it is important to understand that the walls defining each religion are all artificial and seek only to serve the construct of the message that fits into the scope of the presenter's human mind. We are all taught that spiritually enlightened leaders are "not of this world" and there is a certain amount of reverence that should always be used around these leaders of our past. The truth is they are all around us. The amount of reverence required to discuss the subject far exceeds the perception of irreverence.

June 17, 2013

1:30 a.m.

As the experience began, I found myself running through a building. I dropped down to the dirt floor lobby where I knew I had to get back to the room I left. I had just experienced an encounter with an angelic being though its recollection was hazy. I took the stairwell back up. I darted through the third floor hallway. An uneasy feeling about the floor set in. Fear. I got to the end room and I saw a person welcoming me. When I stopped, I realized it was a mirror. I turned around and saw two people cresting over the cubicle walls of their desks behind me. One in particular looked like the person in the reflection. I asked what she wanted with me. She said "it wasn't [her]." I looked to the right and saw a room. I walked in. One of the girls shouted, "Hey! Someone stole my nuts." I shouted back, "It wasn't me, but someone stole my nuts too." When I walked into the room I asked the

Rebirth I

two beings who they were and if they had been stolen from too. One lady was black with short shaved hair. She looked familiar. As she began to tell me I knew who they were, I lost my bearings. I started seeing bright light and flashes of images of impoverished children – young babies it seemed. Childhoods flashed before me. I could not hang on.

In a subsequent vision, I saw two ladies siting in chairs. The room was dimly lighted. I still had fear, but found calm in the room. It was the second time I had been in that building.

June 26, 2013

I felt the whirlwind during the ascent to the heavens. This happened multiple times, but I could not hold onto the moment. It was almost like I was experiencing failed launches. Eventually, I heard Bryan call out to me and ask if I was there. I said I was. I asked him if he had any major projections. He told me with the spirit of a child about the "amazing visuals" from his encounter. He said he didn't see anyone, or speak with anyone, but had a spectacular light-show. He explained it as an aurora and impressed the image to me. I told him I had something similar with a few false starts. So, mine was more of an awareness of nothing. I texted him the next day and said, "Am I to assume that you had an amazing light-show last night, but not a full projection?" to which he replied "How'd you know?! It was like surfing through a nebula. I just stared at it in wonder." I proceeded to tell him that his spirit spoke to

The Written

me about it last night. We locked the time down perfectly within an hour of possibility confirming we were both in flux at the moment.

Also, I had dialogue with God. I asked for guidance with next steps in my career during a prayer spoken out loud while I was driving. The spoken prayer was interrupted when I received a phone call from a former client named Nicholas who wanted to let me know that his employer and he had chosen to part ways. He was such a good soul and deserved goodness to happen for him. In that moment, I realized there was no hope in my career. He was the one person for whom I worked harder than any other to help find a new job, only to have the circumstances not pan out for him. I realized God was answering my prayer through the phone call I received. It gave me definition in understanding whether it was time to move on to all that God has in store for me, or stay behind with my current employer where hope seems lost even in helping others.

Later at lunch, I had a great spiritual conversation with Chad. During that time he described me as "being very technical, and a mental gypsy." He also said I needed to make a clean break from my current position. I returned to work. I spoke with Alex about those thoughts. Upon getting back to my desk, I had confirmation on a placement. This was a spiritual dialogue.

Rebirth I

June 27, 2013

Bryan had his grand encounter with God and "the girl." In the experience, Bryan kept asking what he was supposed to write, where was he supposed to start. God responded by telling Bryan that he amuses Him. He explained that, "Life is like writing. You put the pen down where ever you feel and lift up when you feel inclined to stop." He also asked Bryan how old he was. Bryan responded "thirty-seven." God responded by saying, "Multiply that by seven." God also told him his name was Talon. Bryan was confused to hearing that He had another name other than "Bryan." As he tried to sort out the conversation, "the girl" said, "I don't think he gets it." God and "the girl" snickered. She pulled Bryan from his body so he could see what he looked like. He was floating with feathered wings.

...

Thinking about the comment from Chad yesterday about defining what I do (Jonathan, Inc.), I determined I was a carpenter of modern times. I take a thought – an abstract – and use all of the available technical tools at my disposal to bring it to fruition. Programming languages and skill sets are just my tools. Some people identify as the tool or utensil in their careers (a.k.a. woodworkers as programmers). But, now I was coming to understand how skill sets are analogous to tools and I am merely a carpenter. In all I do, I attempt to inspire and provide hope. This is the role of the artisan in the carpenter.

The Written

Also, today I prayed out loud about needing help understanding through the noise. Due to my heightened awareness of the spiritual dialogue, I politely asked God to shout at me because I may have difficulty sifting through the noise (over-analyzing, etc.). I received an offer immediately upon arrival at work, but it was not what I expected. It resulted in me using a tool in my belt – not all of the tools. But as the day wore on, I realized there were no other distractions that arose at all, which was highly unusual. It was in the recognition of the unusual calm in the day that I realized that by me asking God to shout, there was actually a silencing of the noise around me so I could hear the one simple Voice in the silence. Through that Voice, I heard the call to act on an opportunity I was presented with earlier in the day. This is the day my career would change directions.

June 28, 2013

As I sat down in my bed tonight and turned out the lamps on either side of the bed, the moonlight engulfed the room. I realized there was a presence in close proximity to me. This presence was warm and peaceful. I knew it was angelic. I paused, waiting for the seemingly impossible to happen. I was not sure if an angel was going to materialize in front of me or if it was I that had to figure out how to see. I sat at attention in my bed for several minutes. Eventually, I began speaking out loud to it, letting it know I was aware of the presence and

Rebirth I

wanted to see it. I sat quietly, listening for anything. I tried to focus without focusing my eyes. Suddenly, my attention was drawn to a shelf along a wall adjacent to my bed. The shelf is made of 1x1 cubbies arranged in a 5x5 grid. The moonlight pouring in the window illuminated part of the shelf. The glow was strange – more peculiar than usual. I knew the presence was there and it was up to me to be able to see it. I allowed my eyes to drift in and out of focus of the shelf, and eventually found the point of focus on the undefined. The shelf warped and distorted in perspective in ways I have never before seen. The moonlight illuminated the shelf dividers and, as my focus changed, the distortion became more pronounced. The presence was aware I had located it, but also acknowledged I was not quite ready to see it. It dissipated. No more distortions even though the moonlight was still pouring through the window illuminating the same parts of the shelf. I decided it was time for bed, so I said my prayers – during which I acknowledged the presence and asked for help in learning how to see it.

June 29, 2013

Tonight I was taken into the heavens. Many of the same familiarities existed, but I could tell I was in a more divine location this time. "The girl" was there to greet me and, in usual fashion, guide me through the journey. However, this time was different. This time, she appeared in what I can only describe as her true, divine form. In previous encounters, she was always slightly shorter than me. This time, she stood somewhere in the neighborhood of thirteen and fifteen feet tall – assuming I was still my normal height of approximately six feet tall. She walked on my right side where there was a profound significance placed upon the symbolism of the right side. At times she held my hand. I felt like a small child walking with an adult. When we held hands, I had to reach my hand up around the height of my head to hold hers.

We walked for hours through Heaven. She told me the secrets of the universe, the story of how we came into existence, our purpose, place and reason for being. She told me all of this as we casually strolled through the Heavens. The surroundings were never in focus for me. I was locked into a childlike gaze at her as she told me everything I ever needed to know. The path on which we walked was fluid in creation. It continued to expand outward as we walked. The path was like a golden road – but closer to a fluid light than a physical material. At times, the path was lined with a silver curbing that was flush and defined the edges of the golden road. The surroundings were varied throughout the conversation, but there was one moment I noticed grass and hills that were so green that the color would be impossible to describe on Earth. Most of the time, though, the surroundings were dimmed and only the immediate area we were standing upon was illuminated. Often times, outside of the illumination, I was only aware of darkness with little to no definition.

Rebirth I

Her words were eloquent and motherly. Her attention to the stories and how she communicated with me could be equated to how a parent tells grand stories to a child – careful to maintain the imagination and wonder, but eloquent enough to flatter the intelligence.

There came a point about an hour into our time together that I became extremely excited. It was the moment I realized the gravity of the moment, and the passive amazement faded away. Like a child wanting to open presents on Christmas, I asked if I was going to get my name. I referenced Bryan's great encounter from before, and how I was so excited because I did not think this moment would actually come. She laughed a lot, giggling to herself. I could tell I was amusing to her in some childlike way. I somehow knew the walk she had taken me on had more importance. We were on the way to speak with God. As we continued to walk, and she carried on with her stories, I continually asked when I would learn my name. "Excited" was an understatement in describing my emotions in that moment. In all of the questions, even with the awareness of knowing that we were going to speak with God, something I said eventually caused her to share the most important thing she had to share with me.

While all of the other stories she shared were communicated in a manner that we would communicate on Earth, this moment was different. She sent a swirling message of duality to me – infinitely more difficult to understand, but critical in the moment. While it is impossible to put this kind of communication into words, I can only describe it as a swirly thought….or like a rubberband. In the message, she told me that I was not going to be able to learn my name just yet, but there was a reason. And whatever the reason was (she did not say), she told me I was in the right place, and in time I would understand all that she was saying – and I would know; in fact, I already did know, but I would not be able to recall it yet. There was a strong emphasis on the timeframe of a week passing before I was to tell Bryan about the experience. I have no idea what it was in reference to, though. There were also instructions to write, though it was not discussed in depth – just the commandment to write. It was as if she knew my spirit was not yet old/strong enough to make it much longer on our stroll. Perhaps that is why I was told that it will happen soon.

Suddenly, the presence of God formed to her right. My excitement shot through the roof in anticipation of learning my name, my identity. Somewhere in this moment my body overheated and I flashed out of Heaven and into the region somewhere between Earth and Heaven. Here I wrestled with all of the information I had learned. The secrets to the universe and all of the stories she shared with me were placed in the back of my mind as I focused on discerning the rubberband thought. For nearly another hour I focused on the thought, but had no further clarity. I eventually came back down to Earth.

Rebirth I

June 29, 2013
4:00 a.m.

I was walking around somewhere between Earth and Heaven. It seemed like an exercise in futility, but I wandered around seeking out the voice – calling out, "Hello." I saw buildings, cars (though no one seemed to be driving them), other people, and cobblestone roads. The first time I walked through this area, I went about all of the activities, mostly walking, listening intently without ever hearing the voice. The second time, I thought I heard the voice calling me home. The third time, I took the same path (North to West to South to East) and I finally heard the voice in the distance. It was only a glimmer, but enough to lead me to my next destination.

When I finished the exercise, I told "the girl" who was waiting for me that I heard the voice. She seemed surprised – almost as if she did not believe me. She told me to try again. I took the same path one more time. As I turned to go West, I heard the voice as plain as day. It sounded like a loud whisper calling out my name (Jonathan). I shouted out, "What?" The reply was, "This way." I began heading in a diagonal path northwest where I kept looking behind me expecting "the girl" to show up, but she did not. The voice was omnipresent. I continued to follow her directions. One time, she told me to stop – which I did – right before a car came whizzing by me from North to South. I was smiling, joyous, overcome with the moment. She led me to a building with an awning of sorts. I

The Written

stood under it and I heard the voice one more time, louder and clearer than ever. The voice said, "Good job! That was such a good job." I replied, "I know!! I told you I heard the voice. I tried to explain it the last time and I didn't think you believed me." She said, "No, that was a really good job." As those words rang out, she appeared in the distance, walking over the line of the horizon toward me. The horizon was close though (not like on earth). When she reached me, she gave me a big hug and then I came back to Earth. North was out, out was down, but down was straight ahead. Also, "the girl" was taller than me, but not as tall as from the other day. I would perceive that to be recognition in my growth, or her not wanting me to flip out about her height and maintain the status quo.

After returning to Earth and writing about the experience, I realized that the voice was a metaphor, and the spiritual voice I felt like I was hearing was becoming more noticeable… much stronger like how it appeared in my earthly walk during the week before. As an example, remember the dialogue I had with God about my next steps (the call about Nicholas on 6/26 and the placement after I told Alex I would). My experiences are continuing to further my spiritual growth in the heavens and on Earth. My response to the angel stating, "See I told you I heard the voice," was the same as me saying it the other day in the dialogue with God. The truth she offered though, was that I did not hear the voice as clearly as I did on my last pass.

Rebirth I

Later in conversation with Bryan, he talked about having a bad day. Somewhere in the dialogue he mentioned a doctor who had an unusually bold voice coming into the emergency room that day during his shift. The man talked to him about Aikido and a new class in town. They talked for an hour about the spiritual side of aikido which attracted the ears of all of the others in the ER. Bryan's martial arts friend was in the ER as well and made the introduction between Bryan and the doctor – even though they had spoken just prior. In the moment, he missed the importance. But in our conversation, he realized the importance. Even the boldness in his voice – the physical embodiment of the spiritual voice in that instance – was glossed over. Bryan sees the obvious more than I do, but I see the details more. He does not see through the noise as well as he needs to (nor do I, but this is just a comparison of strengths and weaknesses). Bryan also talked to me about the significance of arriving back at the girl in the East (approaching the East in terms of masonry). We also talked about the symbolism in nearly being hit by the car.

And, though this is from the previous day, I forgot to write it down. In that particular conversation with Bryan, we talked about me possibly never meeting a girl that was my spiritual counterpoint. At lunch, Sam talked about how much I have changed over the last year... dramatically so. Even in answering questions that she once asked a year ago when we first met and how I answer those very same questions today have changed. One example she gave was my answer to the question if I would ever remarry. Apparently, my answer is remarkably different. We talked about our chemistry, the recognition in seeing the spiritual bond and acting on that physically. But, we were both strong enough to see through it. Over the last night, I was impressed that I would meet my spiritual counterpoint. She would embody a very strong earthly chemistry – both sexually and physically – and be a wanderer like myself. She would likely have made the journey alone and would be a spiritual firecracker of sorts. I can see an image of her – long brown hair, petite, shorter, small frame, marches to the beat of her own drummer. She wore sunglasses in the image, but I can see her eyes. It left me unsure of the color of her eyes. She would be on a similar spiritual level as I but will have made it without help. She will perhaps not even have family. I see her completely in a world of her own on this Earth. She will be used to having conversations with God and "the girl" on a very regular basis. She will also help me grow much like Bryan has so far. The harmony will be grand. I was impressed to re-watch the movie "I Am Number Four" to see this type of relationship in action. Bryan says I have my divining rod in full working order. And, that now, I am divining the voice more fluidly than ever before. I would agree.

June 30, 2013

I really have no words to describe last night. The best I could do is to attempt to relay the experience, but clarity and definition will be lacking. I journeyed somewhere between

Rebirth I

Earth and the heavens. I have very little way of describing it other than being engulfed in a great amount of energy. The view was spectacular – a spectacle of colors and brilliant flashes of light. All I could do was soak it all in, eyes full of wonder. Though I have experienced flashes of light before, this was different, almost as if I was not unique to my body, but part of something greater. I was spoken to the whole time while I was in this flux. But, the words were not audible.

Much like the previous experience, the thoughts were impressed to me in that swirly, rubberband-like fashion. While this type of thought is nearly impossible to put into words, I can say that the thoughts were comforting. The overall theme would best be described as, "Everything is okay. Everything will be okay. You are where you are supposed to be." I am sure that the words apply to my earthly walk in addition to my spiritual journey, but most importantly were impressed to me in order to help me maintain my stability while in flux.

The flux was glorious, though such a different experience than any other journey I have taken away from the Earth. To begin to explain the experience would be futile, for it is unlike any earthly experiences could relate. Even the most imaginative minds would not be able to understand the moment this experience becomes real. For some time, Bryan has spoken of such places and experiences. To his credit, he has described them in an amazing manner that I could envision.

It is only for this reason, I have to believe that my experience was of similar gravity to the experiences he has previously experienced in the flux-like state. Imagine taking a journey

The Written

through a nebula, all brilliant in color, that is constantly transitioning in form like the clouds against the blue sky background, brilliant flashes of a rainbow light bursts seemingly randomly, appearing. Now imagine instead of being a person experiencing it, imagine you are part of the energy, but uniquely able to discern your individuality as well as recognition of the whole. That is about the best I can describe it.

July 2, 2013
4:00 a.m.

I was in recognition that I was in my bed, tossing and turning. I rolled over and realized my discomfort and attempt to sleep paralleled with my life's journey. In one glorious moment, I became aware of the super path. I immediately was not in my body. I was laying on my back, realizing I was instantly in the backseat of a cab sitting up. There was a girl driving. She turned around and said she needed to change her plans, that she was hungry. We were close to my place, but I instantly said, "Okay." I realized the path was constantly moving. We went into a restaurant where she and her friend made a comment about a person of importance being in the restaurant. The person's name was "Daniel." I wandered if it was the Biblical Daniel or if my spiritual name might be Daniel. Perhaps, I am Daniel? It is a question that needed to be asked whether it was true or not.

Rebirth I

My body tossed on Earth and the path changed again. I became accepting of every change to the path, because it all had purpose. With each change, new situations presented themselves. Just a slight motion, or a thought – acceptance I was in the flow of the river was all it took. I found joy. I knew this super path was the Spirit and demonstrated the ebb and flow in life. The girl's voice would periodically fill my mind – asking, instructing. I merely listened and acknowledged. I was happy. I was told the name of my path was "the super path," and it flowed around us like a river. I became excited and realized I needed to write down this moment.

As I tried to return to Earth, I found myself somewhere between here and there where I thought I was back in my residence. Bryan was in the distance. I began writing feverishly, recalling all of the details vividly. I relived the memory of the adventure. I asked Bryan how his night went and he said, "Oh. Lots to talk about." I kept writing. I turned to him again and said, "So I guess no trips to heaven?" He said, "That's not what I said. I said we have a lot to talk about." I realized it was absurd I was talking to Bryan as I wrote because he lives another state away. It was at this moment that I realized I was not in my bed, but somewhere between the spiritual playground and Earth. I forced myself back to Earth to write this down. The memories are now not as vivid, but I am recounting them again (for the second time).

Also, there was a point I tried to readjust my body and pulled a muscle in my knee. There were multiple incidents of this and pain. They did not last long. The were just quick experiences of tinges of pain. I realized they were necessary redirections. I fully obeyed and now my body is fine. Upon re-entry, there were still remnants of the pain. Also, some of the redirects were health oriented.

As I would come to find out in conversation later in the day, Bryan had the same experience as I. His involved a cube shape while in a box. He also experienced constant redirections. Eventually, he opened the box where he breathed in the golden dust inside. He also ran five miles in sprints the following morning on Earth after being invigorated by his travels to the heavens.

July 7, 2013
5:00 a.m.

I have had three nights of visions, but without real definition. They were all rubberband-like visions that left me confused. This last one though included me playing a round of golf in a foursome. We were all standing around the green ready to play our balls. I had to chip one onto the green. I was successful and holed it in. I immediately was approached by "the girl." She seemed to want to interview me about the tournament and congratulated me on how well I played. I apparently surprised the field with my play. I was extremely confused because, while I knew I was playing golf, I could not remember the previous 17 ½ holes. After the "interview," I asked the other players in my foursome (who all were veterans

Rebirth I

or famous, though not in a way I knew on Earth) how long we had been playing. They were confused at my question, but told me we had played a whole round of golf. All I could seem to put into words was how confused I was. I knew we were "being filmed" (hence the interview by the girl) so this was not in relation to that, but all I could liken my confusion to was "being in a movie." This was my attempt at explaining the spiritual concepts from Inception – realizing the dream had no beginning – and how we were acting with a force upon me so it must be a dream. But all I could ever say was, "I feel like I'm in a movie or something. You know? Like I just can't remember anything prior to the last few moments."

July 7, 2013

On the car ride from Saint Simons Island to Atlanta, my daughter, Georgia, became aware of the way the music we were listening to was synced with the environment around us. One of the song's main lines in the chorus was "Close your eyes." Every time that line was sung, we went under a bridge. She said, "Daddy, this song is so weird. Every time it says close your eyes, we go under a bridge. It's like a future song or something." I asked her to keep explaining. She continued to elaborate on why she was calling it a "future song."

The next song began to play. It too appeared to have the lyrics synced with events around us. She pointed it out again. I told her that I was extremely proud of her for noticing. I explained to her in the best childlike terms I could muster, how everything in the world is working with everything around us. I told her that what she was beginning to recognize was the fabric of life. I explained that, like fabric is woven, so are all of the events around us. I told her that most people would never notice, but she was already becoming aware of it. She thought about what I said for a minute and then said, "Daddy, it is like there is a king and queen somewhere telling us what to do through everything around us, but we are already doing what they are telling us to do." I told her how happy I was and how that very concept meant far more than she realized. I didn't elaborate (since I didn't want to overwhelm her) but she was significantly in tune with the events of the moment.

After dropping off Georgia, I stopped to fill up gas in my Jeep. For some reason, I decided I needed to clean the interior of my windows. Seeing as I had never done this outside of a carwash, it was an unusual thought, but I proceeded – carefree with the time. A car pulled up next to me and immediately a lady got out. She was Caucasian, a bit overweight and had very poor skin complexion. She came up to me instantly and asked me if I had a dollar or two to spare. She then began to explain something about why she needed the money, but I stopped her and told her I did not carry any cash on me. She apologized and immediately got on her cell phone to call someone for help. I felt terrible in the moment. I have always been cautious with people who approach me soliciting for money. But something inside of me told me this was different.

Rebirth I

I also felt guilty because I had lied. I actually had a $10 bill on me, but I was holding onto it in case of emergencies.

I sat in my Jeep, ready to leave and noticed the large change pile on my console. I realized there must be a couple dollars in change so I scooped it up and then gave it to her. She thanked me and I left. As I was driving away, I prayed to God aloud. I apologized for judging the woman and her needs. It was as if I needed to know I was giving her money for a certain purpose. I realized I was wrong and that my inner voice had queued me in. I told God that I would act differently from then on in those situations.

I questioned if I did not give the $10 out of selfishness, or whether I should have given the lady 10x the amount she asked me for (since that was all of the cash I had on me). I was not sure what the right decision should have been, but felt content since I had given her all of the change in my car. Even so, I still felt that I lacked in execution of responding to the spirit. I decided that from then on, if I could help in any capacity (regardless of my perceived purpose of why something was needed), then I will willingly do so, for I am merely a vessel blessed with the fruits of the spirit. If someone asks for help and I have extra fruits, then I should help satisfy that call. Even the wicked who may have bad intentions are actually crying out for help. In the end, my effort is fuel for the spirit – a catalyst for good – so I should not question, but merely recognize my purpose in the moment.

A few miles down the road, I stopped at Wendy's for dinner. Upon completing my order at the drive thru, I was asked

The Written

to donate a dollar to help in the search to cure cancer. I typically say no to any "add-ons" or "fundraisers" offered as an addition to a purchase I am making. Again something was different in this moment. The cashier took the time to describe what the $1 would be used for and had something extra in his voice – something that my spirit identified. To someone else, he may have sounded like he stumbled and fumbled in his delivery of the use of the $1. To my ears, I heard his inner voice attempting to override his motor functions and deliver a specific message to me.

I immediately replied that I would donate a dollar. Whether this was just a coincidence, or God reaching out again, it didn't matter. I had just prayed that I would be different upon recognition of His voice asking for assistance, so I listened. If it was a coincidence, this was still my moment to make amends for my original slow reaction time to the lady at the gas station. As I left, I prayed aloud again echoing my confusion on the intended use of the $10 of cash in my wallet, but saying that I heard His message this time. I was extremely happy to have made whole my contribution to the request for a couple of dollars from earlier.

So, if two times still has the possibility of coincidence, three times is absolutely God's signature to occurrences in my life. Somewhere down the road – maybe an hour after I picked up my dinner – I exited off to stop and go to the bathroom. While I rarely stop at Wendy's, it was the only place on the exit, so I pulled in. This was the second stop at a Wendy's in an hour. I pulled into a parking spot a car had just left. As I

Rebirth I

parked, I noticed the car that had previously just backed out, had begun to pull forward and was now at a complete stop just a few feet ahead of the parking place. As I opened my door to get out a lady was standing at my door. She had apparently been in the car that had just pulled out. This lady was African-American, overweight, and had poor skin complexion. She reminded me instantly of the woman from the gas station. Her eyes held within them a certain amount of hope directed toward me.

She apologized for having to ask me for anything, but began to explain that nobody in the parking lot would help her family and that she just needed $10 or $20 dollars to help them get home. Now, I've been solicited for money many times in my past, but never have I been solicited for that much at a time. Immediately I recognized my prayer on the $10 and knew in the moment that God was again giving me another opportunity to confirm that I heard his voice. This time, though, it was direct. He asked for me to give the amount of cash I had in my pocket. I stopped the lady before she could finish explaining why she needed it. I told her, "All I have is $10 cash, but that she could have it." She was extremely gracious and began to head back to her car while thanking me. I looked at her and out of nowhere I said, "Please use that for what you asked."

The words that left my mouth were not delivered from my brain. I believe wholly that the voice of God, came across my lips giving direction to the lady. For what purpose she needed the money, I will never know. More importantly, I do not

The Written

need to know. In that moment, God spoke to me through her and to her through me. I acknowledged the recognition of His voice and the use of my body and fruits for His purpose. The lady may never know why she chose to stay in the parking lot and make the effort to approach me after exhausting all options and clearly attempting to leave. To her, she could have chalked it up to any number of reasons. She may not even recognize the exchange that took place. But, God is working on her, just as he is working on me. It is not my place to question or cast judgment on anyone's situation. She had a need for money, regardless of the circumstances that brought her to that point, or the results of her use of the $10 afterwards. One day, maybe she will look back and see He was there all along, protecting her. Maybe it will not happen that easily. But in any case, when the words fell across my lips instructing her to "please use [the money] for what she asked," she paused in recognition, her face radiating spiritual recognition in a mortally confused expression. She replied, "Oh absolutely." And in that moment, the work of God was enacted and further growth of all parties involved were set into motion.

July 8, 2013
5:30 a.m.

I was picked up with another person and being driven to a house. In the front seat was a man of divine stature. To his right, was an assistant (who seemed more like the catalyst for

Rebirth I

the guy). Eventually, conversation became more fluid and the main guy said something about how he didn't like country music these days – that something has been lost in the music.

We stopped at a building. He explained that he once was in a building like this in another country. He explained that he Loved it so much, he had immediately asked for the architect and had one built in this present location. We all walked inside. I did not hesitate to push the envelope with this guy. He walked ahead of us, I rushed forward and began explaining why I thought country music had faltered. I explained that digital music had added so much detail and definition, that the human element no longer existed. I also mentioned that songs have become commercialized instead of written from the heart. I told him I expected that songs would get better soon because we were in a cyclical state.

Inside the building, he wandered down a stairwell that curved down and to the right. I followed. About a level down, he pointed out the bathroom. I went in to make use of it. When I came out, I walked upstairs into a room. There was a younger guy, familiar in appearance, sitting on a chair. Another man quietly sat in the adjacent room. The younger man was playing guitar. He was obsessed with how it sounded and so intrigued that someone from the Flaming Lips had played it before. I wandered through the adjacent room, through an open double doorframe and over to a piano. My deceased Uncle Gary came in. He sat down at the piano and began playing. My mom walked in. They started reminiscing about the past.

Gary told my mom how much Gayle had been the glue for Steve after they met (their brother and his wife). I heard a story of how Gayle once carried eight separate drums out to the car for Steve when he wanted to purchase a new set. They laughed and enjoyed the moment. Eventually, Gary asked my mom to play the piano. He said, "It has been so long and we don't get the chance to see each other often. Can we play a song together?" My mom was bashful and apologetic for not knowing anything new, but she played anyway. They sat down together and began playing a song. I watched the rise and fall of the hammers on the strings. The place Gary sat had more hammers than a typical piano, and his music was gorgeous. I awoke.

July 11, 2013

Today Bryan shared with me a major moment with him and "the girl." These are the notes I took of his experience:

In the beginning of the experience, Bryan continued to hear "whizzing sounds" pass his head. These sounds startled him and caused him to wake up. As he went back to sleep, he began seeing blobs of blue light. This is common before his ascent to the heavens. As the blue lights came into focus, he arrived in the heavens. He found himself in a classroom. The teacher and another person were talking. He knew they were talking to him, but it did not matter to Bryan. He knew something was off, but just assumed he was in a real classroom. He

Rebirth I

observed a desk that seemed more like a protrusion from the wall than a desk we would know on Earth. There were also two sets of file drawers on either side. He described them as pillars.

Bryan realized he was sitting in a chair in the classroom. His gaze fell upon the window where he could see a cobblestone street outside. It was familiar – a city that we have described in past conversations as "Thomas Kinkaid-like." There was a purple hue to the street. It was wet and had the appearance of humidity, though he sensed the temperature was more like that of a cave. He began to hear noises – dinner sounds on plates and ambient voices. He also came to realize he had gained tactile sensations. The realization of his senses caused him to turn his attention back upon the classroom where his gaze fell upon the chalkboard.

At the front of the class there was a person writing symbols on the chalkboard. Turning to look at the class, he realized that the class was divided in a back-to-back style. Mindi was sitting on the front row. Bryan waved at her to grab her attention. She waved back.

Upfront, a male angel took his place on the left side of the classroom. A female angel took her place to the right side. On the left, Bryan noticed an empty picture frame. It was made of old palette wood to create the appearance of trim. A woman with dark hair walked up to Bryan and greeted him. She said that it had been a long time and proceeded to ask if he was dating anyone. Bryan said "no" but indicated that he was just talking to someone…not dating. The brunette made a comment about a time in the past that she and Bryan had shared together in the basement. Bryan could not recall her memory, but played along. The brunette went on to say that Mindi wanted to talk to him.

At this point, our granddad walked through the door and placed a clear plastic envelope on the desk in front of Bryan (measuring about two inches by two inches). Granddad tapped the envelope with two fingers as if to draw attention to a certain importance, then he turned and walked out. Inside of the bag were pills with the word "VITA" printed on them. Bryan told him, "I Love you." as he walked through the door.

The teacher approached Bryan after our granddad left. Bryan said, "That's my grandfather. He's a wonderful man." The teacher smiled and then took Bryan through the doorway and told him that now it was time for him to tell her the answer to a question. "What question?" Bryan asked. Puzzled by the question, Bryan then took notice of a song playing in the background with the words, "She's the one." He didn't quite understand the randomness of the moment until he heard a person next to him say, "He still isn't quite here. We are going to have to turn it up." Bryan realized the song was supposed to be a queue for him to recognize "the girl" despite her appearance being different. Instead, they had to resort back to the visual queues that he would recognize during his journey.

At this moment, a drawer to his bottom left opened up and a radio that was his father's flew out of it and made a loud boom on the floor. This awoke Bryan from the dream and brought him into lucidity. The dark-haired girl said, "I won-

Rebirth I

dered when you were gonna wake up. I really wanted to talk to you." This time in appearance, "the girl" appeared as a brunette instead of blonde. I believe this to be one of two girls, but both hold a similar heavenly significance to us.

She guided him outside on a cobblestone street. There was a trash-hopper filled with beautiful rocks with a length of rope laying next to it. Someone stood behind Bryan (disjointed). She asked him to explain what he saw in regard to the hopper, the rocks, and the rope. Bryan began to explain concepts that transcended his own knowledge:

...

"To pull or push the cart of rocks would make the cart move. The push was ego. The pull was the way. The rope was help, and is initially taught until a person gains dominion over the natural forces. After it becomes taut, to keep it taut will end in destruction. When the rope is loose, yet held onto, the cart is unaware of intentions, but understands the dominion."

...

He realized in that moment he was teaching as well as being taught. That person may or may not have known he was there, but Bryan was being groomed in that moment in the presence of his own teacher. The conversation was chiseling down into the concept of Gary speaking across time.

After Bryan and I spoke, I realized I needed to share Gary's recent communication with my mother (Gary's sister). Having never shared anything of this magnitude with anyone other than Bryan, I somehow knew this was the next step on the journey I was taking. For Bryan and me, these conversa-

The Written

tions have become commonplace. However, sharing just a fraction of this type of information with another person could rock their foundation of understanding. Weighing the risks, I still understood I was supposed to speak with my mom. I called her. She was at my sister's.

Everyone had just finished lunch and were lying down for naps (kids, etc.). She had some time to talk and was alone. I began the conversation telling her that I needed to tell her something that was important and that she was going to have a hard time understanding everything, especially without any backstory. I told her I expect her to have questions and I would be glad to answer any of them, but it was important that I share this with her. In retrospect, I am sure she feared the worst – but I really was not sure how to prep someone for the information I was about to drop on them. I led by telling her that I had spoken with Uncle Gary the other day. I stopped to gauge her reaction.

She said, "Gary?" She was obviously confused. I said "Yes. I know this already sounds weird, but please bear with me because it is important I say everything." She said, "Okay…" I proceeded to tell her that I would not be sharing this if it wasn't important, but that Gary had communicated with me and wanted me to convey this message to her. I told her the message would be better understood by me reading the notes I took immediately following my interaction with him. Before I read her the portion of the experience that applied to her, I told her that it was important to understand that if she

Rebirth I

truly believed in the mind/body/spirit, then she would need to understand that my spirit communicated with him.

I explained there are times that the soul resides in the body, and times that it appears to be traveling to other locations. The feeling in the gut – that is the recognition of spiritual communication at its foundation. I then went on to read her the experience in the encounter. She asked a few questions along the way – wanting to know more information such as the song she played on the piano. I answered that it was a song I had never heard before. But for the most part, she listened intently.

After sharing with her the moment, I asked her if she was okay. She said she was, so I continued. I shared with her that what I witnessed was actually her spirit interacting with his, though she probably would not remember. I told her that the house that Gary was in was beautiful and that he was very happy. I said that he wanted to bring harmony to the family, and that it was important that she know he was behind it, though there are others as well. I went on to explain that he is constantly communicating with her and Karen and the other family members in an effort for everyone to remove the barriers and find harmony. He wanted harmony. I told her that I was in Saint Simons Island for a reason over the holiday weekend because I was impressed to go. I knew it was important on a spiritual level, though I did not know why. I just followed His command. I shared with her that even I was not sure why I was down there until the text from Aunt Karen arrived. Only then did I start to see the picture. It was not until after I had

The Written

spoken with Gary and then had the conversation with Bryan that I realized the significance – though I did not include Bryan in the story (to keep it simple).

I told her to think of me as a conduit. I was a link in all of the events that occurred. For whatever reason, being in her presence was important to help the chain of events happen. I explained that I was a gateway to sharing the experience with her because I could see it. I also told her that the text message happened along the same lines – due to my presence in the moment. And by me, I meant my spirit as a conduit. I explained a little more as best as I could. I told her that this was not the first time I had communicated with Gary, but it was the only time I have shared with her because it was the only time I had been directed to tell her. She asked me what he has said in other conversations. I told her that it was not important because the only thing that mattered was what I was telling her now.

She asked me how I felt when it happened. I said, "Every moment when it happens is amazing." I asked her how she felt at this time. She said that it was a lot to take in – that I know she will think about it a lot because that is what she does. I told her "Good. That is what is supposed to happen." I then went on to tell her that if she wanted to talk about it, I would be glad to answer any questions she would have and that I would be available anytime to discuss all that I had shared (for however long she wanted to speak about it). And, if she wanted never to speak of it again, then I would honor that too.

Rebirth I

I told her that the important thing for me was to not try to push the information on her, but rather to serve as the vessel for this message. I could not shape how she chose to use the information, only that I could answer any questions she may have. She asked me a couple more questions about the details of the vision again – clearly trying to comprehend all that was being poured on her. Instead of answering the question directly with my distortion of understanding, I told her simply, "Let me reread it to you again, because I think that is the best way for you to understand it." So I did.

We left the call on a great note. She seemed uplifted, though confused and unsure of what all had happened. She continued to reiterate that it would take a while for her to process everything, but that she wanted to understand. I told her I would be here when she needed me. I also told her this was just one of many experiences, not just with Gary but others. She asked me if I was keeping a journal. I told her "Absolutely." She seemed content, and that is how we left the conversation. I texted her later to check in on her, she said she would keep it in confidence and that she was doing well; that it would take a while to digest.

Upon returning to work, Sam noticed my face was flushed red. She asked if I was hot, and I told her no. I was unaware how red my face was. My head also began to hurt in the frontal area. I never get headaches, so this was unusual, as was the flushed face. I looked in a mirror and was confused – then I realized what had happened. Much like a body overheats when the spirit leaves the body, I had just had a similar en-

The Written

counter. My pulse was only sixty three beats per minute (on the low side of things). I was in a meditative state, even upon my return to work. I realized that the conversation I had just had was not me speaking as much as it was conversation being spoken through me. I knew it in the moment, but it was so meditative that it seemed natural.

I truly believe that my conversation was not my voice alone – maybe not mine at all. I also believe that Gary was there. Maybe he was speaking. Maybe he was just latched on to me as a conduit. Either way, the symptoms I had when I returned reflected a metaphysical contact – though more extreme than I have ever had… which would make sense, seeing as this was the first person I had shared this type of information with (aside from Bryan) as well as due to the gravity of the conversation and various forces/souls working through me.

July 12, 2013

Today was my last day at Vaco. It came without fanfare, without announcement, without acknowledgement to anyone else. The experience in this transition has been one of the most surreal pivots in my life. It was like a breakup with someone you truly Love and Loves you in return – but the circumstances, maybe long-distance or something to that effect – were holding both people back from moving forward. Most of my colleagues will find out about my departure next week, though

Rebirth I

my supervisor has been working with me for several weeks on the transition plans. Since no one has been aware of my impending departure save for a couple of people, there was no traditional going away lunch or recognition. The irony is that I had a going away lunch today anyway – though it was not for me.

A good friend from HealthSpring – the employer that was the biggest part of my professional life and growth – has chosen to move onto another career opportunity in Chattanooga. Teresa was a mother figure, a friend, a professional teacher, and more importantly a spiritual guide for me. We worked together the entire time at HealthSpring where she was my senior in tenure and knowledge, but allowed me the opportunity to advance to the manager position in place of her to enable my growth. Upon my departure, she would take over that position and eventually move into another role internally to allow another person the opportunity to grow into her former management position. Truly, she is an amazing person.

The group of people that met for her going away lunch turned out to be mostly the reunited team members I hired and managed while I was there. There were four former managers of that department including the current one (my first hire), Teresa, and Jim – my former mentor and original boss. He gave me my initial opportunity. Everyone holds a special place in my heart, but I have not spoken to many since my departure. I had a hard time looking back through the pride and chaos that ensued in my own business endeavors upon leaving. I so enjoyed sitting around listening to everyone talk. I

The Written

listened more than spoke, and was always surprised to hear the reminiscing of great moments we shared as a team. The lunch was more of a family reunion than a business going away luncheon.

There were several moments that were brought up that occurred under my leadership. In fact, most of the reminiscing was during the time we all worked together. That was a very special time in my life. My team was a family. Work was enjoyed because we Loved to be together. Though the lunch was not for me, I listened to all of the memories and couldn't help but recognize the significance in the moment. We never had a last lunch with team members when I left, and my current employer was not having a lunch for me. But this lunch was as if I was able to experience a past part of my life with a different spiritual perspective than I had at that time. Time constantly moves forward, but I was granted a scenario in which I was able to experience it a second time and see all of the details I had missed since I was so consumed at that time in my own service to self.

After the lunch we parted ways with hugs. But the bigger symbolic point in the story is that the years ensuing after I left HealthSpring have all been monumental in my personal growth. If someone could have pushed "pause" on my timeline on the last day of my employment at HealthSpring and given me an alternative timeline of four years to grow up through my spiritual puberty and get to the point I am at now, today would be the day that someone un-paused my original timeline and allowed me to continue forward. It was the last

Rebirth I

day at Vaco, and my last day lunch was with my former team from HealthSpring for someone else's going away party. My journey forward started today, and I found closure in the reunion of my former family in the process, while the day for everyone at Vaco was business-as-usual with most everyone unaware of my departure.

I probably have not done a great job explaining the symbolism, but truly it means more to me than words can express. It is somewhat of a spiritual seven-and-seven in recognition of me righting the ship that had become lost in the storm for a couple of years. I returned to the office to collect my things and say my goodbyes to the handful of people that were aware.

As I left the office, the surroundings were filled with silence. It was not as if the world was silent for others, it was just that my spirit had muted the world around me. I could see everything around me and the fingerprints of God. Nature was at its most glorious peak of the summer as my eyes witnessed every intricate miracle around me. I decided to drive away in silence – no music, no speaking aloud. I ran a couple of errands where each interaction with another person radiated joy and happiness. It was not as if I was excited in the moment. It was a spiritual recognition of the voice of God speaking through others.

If for a moment, you could imagine a welcoming party waiting to greet your entrance, I witnessed God's welcoming party in the ways that I have learned to recognize so far. The world around me became puppets for God's voice. Everything

The Written

was subtle but in grand splendor. After my final errand, I decided to listen to a few songs Spotify had recommended for me, but I had not heard before. I rolled down my driver side window and let the wind blow through my hair. The song volume was not loud – it was more-or-less intended to be just mood music in the background.

Eventually I came to stop at a red-light. As I sat there, the world became silent around me again even though the radio was playing and cars were passing by. To me, there was an acute sense of focus on my spiritual awareness. For some reason, I felt compelled to glance at my elbow that was sitting on the lip of my doorframe, hanging just over the side. Something gray caught my eye. I noticed a butterfly was sitting on my elbow. I moved my elbow to see if it would stay (knowing it would because of what I am about to say). The butterfly held strong. In the midst of traffic, the butterfly found me. It was subtle in beauty. It was gray with deep blue spots on it's wings with a few fine black lines creating subtle streaks along the grain of each wing. Its body was larger than other butterflies. It was big enough that I stared at it enamored. I knew in this moment, the silence around me, that this butterfly that landed on my elbow in the midst of five lanes of traffic was a part of a bigger message. Whether the butterfly was an angelic soul materialized in the form of a butterfly, or if the butterfly was just a symbol alone, I felt the significance in the moment.

My journey through the last several years had been arduous. My recent employer was a helping hand, reaching out to give me a chance to catch my breath. I had acknowledged

Rebirth I

God's path before me. I did not question, I just listened and followed His guidance.

The butterfly is a creature that experiences a beautiful metamorphosis from caterpillar to insect of flight. It can be one of the most meaningful symbols on the spiritual journey – similar to an angel getting its wings. It is also a symbol that is written about in near death experiences and other people's spiritual encounters. Many have experienced "flying on wings of a butterfly." So as I studied the butterfly, my spirit became flushed in recognition. I smiled at the butterfly to acknowledge I knew and understood. The butterfly turned to me – and as crazy as it sounds – gave me a nod in recognition and turned to fly away.

The silence around me was penetrated only by the words to the song that had been playing at that time. The song was titled "One of Us" by Dave Barnes. Having never heard it before and paying very little attention to the music prior to the red light, I was unaware of what the words were even referencing. But for this moment, it was unimportant. These words – and these words only – were the only sounds in the moment:

...

"Whoever you turn out to be, you're forever part of me.
You turn me to a father from a son.
All we are, you are. And who we'll be, you'll be.
Love and hurt. Doubt and trust – welcome to being one of us."

...

My eyes filled with tears. It was God communicating to me in words, through the persona of His son, welcoming me to

The Written

the family. It was one of the most emotional moments I have ever experienced. I cried while smiling with joy in my Jeep. In those words was the spiritual acknowledgement of my presence, persistence, and dedication to following His path. I knew July would be a major turning point in my life, but I just did not know what direction I would be heading. At this juncture, I still do not, but I do know that everything is going to be okay. I have heard His voice when He has spoken and followed His leads as they have been presented. Truly nothing could bring me down from the place I am in right now. And this is just the beginning.

July 12, 2013
Footnotes

Bryan mentioned in passing at the end of our conversation that we should not leave behind anything we would not want others to see – such as porn (the example he gave). Random comment. We did not elaborate on it. But it stuck out to me.

July 13, 2013
4:00 p.m.

Today I had a quick vision. I was intent on asking the name of "the girl" I continued to speak to, though I know I have asked her many times before. As I focused in on the question, I appeared in a pub. It was dimly lighted and there were several people sitting around pub-style tables. I asked one person at the first table I came to what the girl's name was. She gestured for me to go to the next table over and told me to ask for "Ms. Julia." I wandered over to the next table where there were four people sitting at the table (three immediately visible). When I got over there I asked them what the name of the girl was and who was Ms. Julia. Immediately, they all stood up in recognition of my question. The three I could immediately see began to step aside for me to reveal the fourth person. They all kept saying "Miss Julia" over and over again as they stood up. But the moment became too powerful and I lost contact. I tried to return, but to no avail. I believe the fourth person was going to either be able to answer the question, or was "Ms. Julia," but I guess I will not know the answer. I have also suffered a headache after waking from this projection.

July 14, 2013

I watched a video of a brunette girl that I noticed had the title of "Juliya" on it. It was highly rated, but she was young and innocent. She kept looking at the camera taking queues as if not wanting to be there.

July 15, 2013

Bryan and I talked about it all realizing that we were being told to think about what we were doing and notice the negatives associated with that dark passenger Mindi had also told Bryan that she thought it was the worst thing on Earth. We both knew that it was not right, but have had a hard time breaking free. In our talk, we realized that this was a necessary step for both of us. We realized that three men were protecting me from "her" until I could get this part of my life under control. It is possibly the last tie that binds our spiritual and mortal bodies to this Earth. Everything else can be controlled. This is possibly the hardest to overcome, but we must move forward.

July 18, 2013

After a couple nights of false launches (overheating, pulsing feeling) due to the half moon as well as the half-waking AP's (looking in the mirror, taking a shower, morning routines, etc.), I decided to try to project during the afternoon. I hit a very strong meditative state, and then I began to zone in and out of consciousness. I was very tired when I lay down to meditate, so it became a constant struggle of keeping my mind aware of the projection. Not much came of it. I remember sitting on a patio along a white concrete divider wall that had tables built into it. A guy on my left who seemed to be friends

Rebirth I

with me would casually strike up conversation, but I could not quite figure out how to respond.

Eventually a Michael Bublé song came on that was so clear that it brought me into the moment. I looked at him and said something to the effect of "Isn't it nice? Have you heard his new album yet?" Honestly, I do not know if I have ever heard his album, or what the song was that was playing in the background – but the song was familiar. I just identified it as Michael Bublé and seemed to know what I was talking about. That is the strange thing about projections – often the consciousness knows things the mind does not. While the song was playing, I saw an album cover in front of me. The cover was black with a blue face. I had never seen it before, but assumed it pertained to the song. The man never acknowledged my comment, so I tried to speak again. This time it was hard to speak and sounded like gibberish. I attribute this to not being fully in control of the moment.

Suddenly, I heard a female voice. I turned. She was to my right, sitting at a computer screen. She called out to me to get my attention, then seemed to not care when I responded. I looked at her and tried to talk. I turned to the guy and excitedly told him she was speaking to me. I asked him what he thought she wanted. Again, all I can convey is that I was extremely excited. I looked at her again as she appeared to try to understand what I had said to her before. The gibberish to me was actually a very scientific, or high-minded talk. She appeared to be looking at a record of me on her screen. She pointed to something on the monitor and said, "Oh. You're an

NTS[insert 3 or 4 more letters here]- member and were also part of the Honors Society." She listed off several other abbreviations which I knew were pertaining to mental abilities. Then she let out a sigh of relief – or comfort maybe – and said, "Not that this makes any sense….."

I replied, "Yes I am." She appeared to know why she was babysitting me with my inability to function on their plane. I felt like a dysfunctional child where my mind was moving faster than the vehicle to communicate. After she began to talk to me again, I became more aware of my presence in the moment, and lost grounding on that plane. I returned to my body.

Now that I have written this, I see similarities in the room Bryan was in during his last classroom projection. I will talk with him tomorrow to confirm what I saw.

July 19, 2013
Further Analysis on July 18th's Experiences

I told Bryan about the projection and he immediately saw the similarities with his classroom projection. He was confident we were in the same place albeit at different points in time. He also became excited about the song I heard because that was the same method used to catch his attention. The song in his projection kept repeating the lyrics "She's the one" but until now, he had not told me that the song was familiar to him. The words were to the tune of "Still the One" by Orleans.

Rebirth I

As we talked, he looked up the lyrics and became stark silent. It was as if the conversation with the angels was still taking place. The song choice in his projection carried meanings in communication. It is similar to how Bumblebee in Transformer movies cannot speak directly. Instead, he pieces together clips of audio from earthly recordings into a sentence. While the whole set of lyrics carries an extremely deep meaning, when placed in the context of his heavenly visit and heard through the perspective of a conversation with an angel, there was one specific line that stood out: "Yes. You are." This line echoed back to his earlier visits to Heaven where Bryan asked, "So I am?" and the reply was, "Yes. You are." Here are the rest of the lyrics. Imagine hearing this being told to an angel from the perspective of a human:

"We've been together since way back when
Sometimes I never want to see you again
But I want you to know, after all these years
You're still the one I want whisperin' in my ear

You're still the one I want to talk to in bed
Still the one that turns my head
We're still having fun, and you're still the one

I looked at your face every day
But I never saw it 'til I went away
When winter came, I just wanted to go wanted to go
Deep in the desert, I longed for the snow

The Written

You're still the one that makes me laugh
Still the one that's my better half
We're still having fun, and you're still the one

You're still the one that makes me strong
Still the one I want to take along
We're still having fun, and you're still the one, yes you are

Changing, our Love is going gold
Even though we grow old, it grows new

You're still the one that I Love to touch
Still the one and I can't get enough
We're still having fun, and you're still the one

You're still the one who can scratch my itch
Still the one and I wouldn't switch
We're still having fun, and you're still the one

You are still the one that makes me shout
Still the one that I dream about
We're still having fun, and you're still the one

Still the one, yeah still the one
We're still having fun, and you're still the one"

Rebirth I

This doesn't mean that song was originally written from this perspective, but instead it indicates the careful choice of a method of communication that Bryan would be able to understand upon reflection of all of the events. With heavenly communication, everything is important and carefully chosen so that we as humans can discern the many depths of meaning in a seemingly simple conversation. The literal is important, but the dimensions of meanings are even more important. The dimensions are available for those who understand, but will not be obvious to those who have yet to come to that level of understanding.

So, after Bryan and I joyfully shared all of the similarities in our visits, he tasked me to see if I could identify the song I heard. I obliged. The only information I was armed with in my quest was that Michael Bublé sang it, and that I had been given the image of an album cover (at least that was what I thought it was). I looked up Michael Bublé albums. Sure enough, there was one album identical to the cover I had been given. At this point, I knew it would be easy for outsiders to assume that subconsciously I had seen this album before, and that it was stored somewhere in the depths of my memory. Even I cannot dismiss the doubt that others may have, but I can assure you that this was the first time I had ever seen this album cover. I had not started listening to any Michael Bublé songs until the last year or so – and those were just the ones on the radio. So, finding the album cover, I decided to see if this was his new album that I mentioned to the guy. It was not. It was released in 2002. I then decided to review the song list. I

The Written

immediately identified the song on the back from the projection. It was "Come Fly With Me."

My excitement rose. But – to be safe, I decided to scan through all of the other tracks before listening to it. The other songs were definitely not the ones I heard, which gave me confidence. As soon as I started to listen to Come Fly With Me, I was immediately re-engulfed in the moment I had in the Heavens. This was the song. The lyrics spoke to me even more. The second verse talks about going to Peru – which is where I intended all year to go during the last week of July, but work prevented me from being able to go. I had never been, but have felt a strong calling to visit the country and the various historic areas there. I knew this song was intended for me. Again, this song was carefully chosen to communicate in the way that we learned Bryan's song communicated to him.

From the perspective of an angel, the words are simply amazing. It turns out the song is originally a Frank Sinatra song – which would be why it seemed familiar to me, though I cannot recall ever hearing it (maybe the chorus in the background of a commercial or something). But, I would never have been able to identify it or have any cues to helping me find the lyrics had it been performed by Sinatra in my visit. Think about the process of arriving at this point of spiritual recognition. Everything is divine. See the lyrics below, and especially explore the chorus.

"Come fly with me, let's fly, let's fly away
If you can use some exotic booze

Rebirth I

There's a bar in far Bombay
Come fly with me, let's fly, let's fly away

Come fly with me, let's float down to Peru
In llama land there's a one-man band
And he'll toot his flute for you
Come fly with me, let's take off in the blue

Once I get you up there where the air is rarefied
We'll just glide, starry-eyed
Once I get you up there I'll be holding you so near
You may hear the angels cheer because we're together

Weather-wise it's such a Lovely day
just say the words and we'll beat the birds
Down to Acapulco Bay
It's perfect for a flying honeymoon, they say
Come fly with me, let's fly, let's fly away

Once I get you up there where the air is rarefied
We'll just glide, starry-eyed
Once I get you up there I'll be holding you so near
You may hear all the angels cheer because we're together

Weather-wise it's such a Lovely day
You just say the words and we'll beat the birds
Down to Acapulco Bay
It's so perfect for a flying honeymoon, they say

The Written

*Come fly with me, let's fly, let's fly
Pack up, let's fly away!!"*

July 20, 2013

Bryan shared with me his most recent visit to the Heavens. During this visit, he saw angels in their true form. It was a revisit from another time earlier, but now he was able to better understand his surroundings. The angels were more defined as expressions of white light. "The girl" that we continually see finally gave her name to Bryan. I had been strongly desiring to ask her, but also had not been sure exactly how to tell someone who has been an amazing host and guide, that I do not even know their name. Well, now I do. Her name is Megazalea (May-guh-zuh-lee-uh). She referred to the angels that he was seeing as "The Phalanx" and instructed Bryan to follow them in a vehicle. She rode with him. At first they were black stick figures, very playful. Then they opened up into rectangular expressions of white light (energy?!). They had few facial expressions. Megazalea kept telling Bryan to go faster and faster. They were suddenly encapsulated in fire – like that of reentry. She laughed a playful laugh as if it was a roller coaster. They then proceeded to do more running and jumping. She took him to a ledge. This was the first time he had experienced a true fear of heights, but the fear was encompassed in agape. She wanted him to jump and trust her. Eventually he did and found himself back on Earth.

Rebirth I

Additional research after the recount of events led me to understand that the word "Azalea" is of Hebrew origin. "Meg" means root, or origin. Pretty interesting…

July 21, 2013

As I drifted off into a meditative state, I quickly realized I was being given a list of all of the angel names that I had encountered, or perhaps would encounter. As the list began to be recited to me, I recited it back. I heard "Auriel, Lialel*, Anael." The voice kept moving forward in the list. I began to repeat back the names. It was then I realized I had never heard of Lialel before. This revelation was so jarring that it caused me to realize I was no longer in a meditative state, but somewhere between here and the Heavens. I immediately lost control and awoke.

After combing through all of the resources available to me, I came to learn that Leilel is the name of an angel written "LYL," which is Hebrew for night. The angel is also known as Layla which, interestingly, corresponds to the lyrics of Eric Clapton's song "Layla."

July 29, 2013

I had a brief vision this morning. I awoke to the sound of my daughter watching TV and I quickly fell back asleep and entered the vision. I was standing in a hallway; a familiar male

The Written

angel was standing next to me. He looked at me and said, "Are you ready?" I must have looked puzzled because I was only just then realizing where I was in that instance. He asked again, "Are you ready?" I said, "Yep. Let's do this."

I was filled with excitement, a faux-confidence, and anticipation. We went inside a set of double doors at the end of the hall. The room was large – extremely open with ceilings that must have been fifty feet tall or greater. In the middle of the room were two large chairs made of a dark leather. They were squared off. They had a modern look to them. "The girl" strolled over to one of the chairs and sat down. She motioned for me to come over. I was somewhat star-struck and speechless (which I have never experienced with any celebrity I have met on earth). The warmth of the Love given off by the girl was enough to cause anyone to stop in his tracks. I walked over and sat in the open chair. She began asking me what I can only imagine were supposed to be simple questions. I know I took my time to answer in order to make sure I formed the words carefully and correctly. I was trying not to appear star-struck. In that moment, I felt confident, yet cautious. I knew that I would not have been able to speak to her if I was not ready, so this was a big moment for me.

Unfortunately, all of our conversation was lost in the afterglow of the encounter. I know we talked for what seemed like forever. She smiled a lot and talked with a seemingly strong admiration of me – though it was in a loving and strengthening way. Near the end of our conversation, the male angel walked over and mentioned something to both of us that

Rebirth I

I identified as indicating our session was about to come to an end. And with that, I awoke.

July 30, 2013
2:26 a.m.

The moment began with me standing in front of a person with folded arms on a table. I was extremely close to the arms and I could recognize their great size – my best guess is the arms of someone ten to fifteen feet tall, probably closer to the latter. As I tried to study the girth of the great arms, the entity recognized my awareness and subsequently removed himself from my vision. Blackness. It was as if it was intentional that he was not to be seen.

This has been occurring quite regularly recently. The clarity of my visions has been clouded with (what I can gather as) empty definition. It would seem that the next steps of my growth are not to involve as much handholding as before. As I was processing these thoughts, I found myself in a large, open room with no one around. I believe the setting to be invoked by the angel whose arms I stood before shortly before. The only thing in the room was a device that appeared metallic. I identified it as a "time machine," though a "transportation vehicle" would probably be a better definition. It was large – like a meat freezer – and had a door on it. This was the second time (at least) that I can recall seeing the device.

The Written

On the right side of the facing to the door, a sign was posted. I could read the top line very clearly. It read, "Prepared for you by someone who cares." This phrase was extremely familiar, though I could not identify why. I tried to read the smaller print below it. Like something from a movie, all of the letters started shifting around, rearranging themselves into other words faster than I could comprehend. At this moment I recognized that I was on the verge of losing my stability in this state. I spun around trying to regain my composure. This has worked before, so I hoped it would help me to gather my bearings. I became aware of the coldness of my surroundings.

The coldness was more like a cool basement in winter (not bitter cold, but just a cold chill). This same temperature recognition has been occurring to Bryan and me for some time now – so it is not a recognition of cold in the way the earthly world stigmatizes it. This cold is just a mental recognition of a change in our spiritual plane. The body tries to compensate for the strange surroundings by warming itself up rapidly (hence the overheating/night sweats many experience in dreams). So as I became aware of this new temperature recognition, I realized I was now walking down a street. Again, this was familiar in setting – a place that I had been before. A voice told me that "the person who cares for me was affecting the interaction I was having." And with that, I returned to my bed.

I am sure this could be applicable on many levels, but in the immediate recognition of Bryan's and my slowdown in vi-

Rebirth I

sions, I believe it was intended (on one level or another) to illustrate the next spiritual steps in our lives. For me, I can only attribute the change in vision formats in an equivalent way of watching a child grow up and move out of the house. The lessons they will learn are critical, but necessary. Mom and dad will be there if needed, but the intent is for them to take their knowledge and go out into the world. The parents do their best to help the child out – mostly behind the scenes or in ways that the child will not comprehend until much later in life. Such is the same in our spiritual walks. I believe that with the butterfly, the song lyrics, the recent career change, the form of whatever definition of enlightenment we have had – that this step is the next in an evolution of steps. The vision was just providing comfort in a way to let me know that the onus is on me now to move forth and grow.

August 11, 2013

I will call last night "The Reminder." For the last couple of weeks I have not had any recallable visions or interactions in the Heavens. Bryan has been having the same lull in astral voyages. Last night, I faced a tough mental challenge of deciding whether to go hang out with old friends from my past. These "friends" were the same people that I removed from my life since I realized they were a negative pull. In retrospect, I realize much of that relationship dealt with my own needs to

The Written

re-center myself and focus on my personal journey. It really had little to do with the earthly relationships.

Regardless, I had continually been asked to go out with them. I decided that it was important for me to just show up, and in that action, my forgiveness for their past actions toward me would be apparent – no words, no apologies… just action. I was extremely torn about the decision, though. Part of my decision hinged on the fact that there would be a lot of drinking among the group – which for me I have almost entirely removed from my life. And with that commonality being removed, I did not want to draw a barrier between those people that I could help. I decided that I would have mostly water with no more than two beers for the whole evening (for the appearance).

While I do not have a strong opinion on alcohol, I just know it was a necessary step for me on my journey, to remove it. I observed it dulls the senses and lessens awareness. Before my journey, an occasional drink was a crutch to escape reality…a place where most people on Earth find themselves. But on my journey, anything that intentionally dulls the senses is a step backwards. So with all of that being said, I met up with everyone for three or four hours and returned home. As I began to fall asleep, I prayed for guidance in these types of decisions and for help in understanding my role. Obviously this next step of my journey involved the "getting out in the world and experiencing it for yourself" stage and interactions. I just found myself a little lost being lead into unknown gray

Rebirth I

areas. I had no problem creating my own gray areas though. Actually, in writing this, that may very well be the answer.

Anyway, not long after falling asleep – the brunette girl appeared. Her eyes....wow....I was speechless. She was sitting at a table in the company of others, smiling and laughing. When she saw me, she welcomed me over to their table. She looked so excited to see me, but maintained a composure that indicated that the impetus was on me to remember who she was. I studied her face, her steelblue-gray eyes, the contour of her facial features. I called out a name, "Mary." She did not respond. I was confident her name was Mary (even though that turned out not to be the case). I garnered her attention and said, "I know who you are. Isn't your last name..." My voice trailed off. I wanted to say the name of an earthly person I knew but I recognized my mind was confusing the experience with my spirit. I changed my question. "I know I know you. It has been so long. It is really so good to see you. How long have you been in Nashville?" She smiled at me and told me, "It is so good to see you too. I've been here around a year." I looked at her, my mind racing as to how to respond. I told her "I wish I had known! We could have been hanging out a lot more regularly." She smiled back with so much Love in her eyes. We talked for a while, though I cannot recall the remainder of the conversation. Eventually we parted ways.

The conversation will probably become clearer throughout my day, but the gist of the moment was that She appeared. This was the brunette girl, one of the angels that is (and has been) interacting in my life. Whether it is Anael or Arielle, I cannot be sure since I have names and faces, but no direct association. It should be noted that I feel extremely confident the brunette is Anael. The brunette started appearing about a year ago in my life, after the blonde angel. Her subtle reminder of being in Nashville "for around a year" was an homage to my personal journey. All in all, just her appearance meant everything to me and answered my prayer for guidance and help in understanding my role.

August 14, 2013

I time-shifted for the first time I could legitimately verify today. We all have experienced déjà vu – and this was definitely not the same experience. There have been times over the last year or so that I thought I had experienced time shifting forward, but had not been able to quantify it beyond "strong déjà vu." Today, I was having dinner and watching football. I was extremely inner-focused to the point that I became aware that I was alive inside my mortal body and the outside world was almost completely muted and hazy. I glanced up at the TV and was extremely confused. The play I had just witnessed was the game kickoff from the NY Jets to the Detroit Lions. The kickoff sailed through the end zone and Matt Stafford was running onto the field to QB for the Lions. So, I would have expected when I glanced up at the TV to see the next play of the game. I did not. In fact, my bearings became really confusing for a split second as I focused on the TV. The game had

Rebirth I

flipped sides of the field and the Jets now had the ball. Their QB threw an interception right to a defensive lineman and he ran it into the end zone. I read the jersey name but only saw a portion of the name. I thought it began ANSAR. I was rattling the name Ansari around in my head. The game went to commercials and when it returned, the Jets were taking the field. This was almost a replay of what I had just witnessed. Then, I watched it all play out again – narrating the plays all along. Though I know I was watching a re-airing of the game, I wanted to take note that it was a "re-airing" and not live... just in case any question to the legitimacy of this journal entry arises.

September 1, 2013

Though the vision was brief, the ramifications are quite grand. I was standing in front of two beings – the one to my right was formless; the one to my left was a woman with seven heads. Perhaps there were more heads – I was not counting the number since the spectacle was already a sight to behold. But nonetheless, this was my experience and my impression at the time was that there were seven heads. As I shifted my vision from the right figure to the left, all of the faces were happy, smiling, and full of excitement. This was not a moment where beauty was conveyed. This was pure anticipation and excitement of this moment I was experiencing. I realized I was asking a question, and I continued to shift my vision from the seven heads to the formless figure. Suddenly, I realized we were involved in a conversation where the two figures were telling me that I had performed a great deed. I humbly played it down, and I asked directly, "What about the sphinx?" I continued to ask and shift my question from one to the next. Both were happy I was asking the question, and seemed pleased that I was unable to answer my own question. It was as if I was being told that the sphinx is the key to the answer I seek. At least – that is the impression I received. Anyway, as quickly as the vision came, it went away. I am now left to ponder the mysteries of the sphinx. (To note, I have never been intrigued or interested in the sphinx. Ancient culture – yes. The sphinx – not once. I always saw it as a symbol, but now it is evident that it holds a greater meaning I must uncover).

After doing some research today regarding the vision, I believe "the deed" to be the understanding of light/sound/energy being intertwined in a compressed space (as found in the Sonalkiss 7 document I recently wrote).

September 15, 2013

I had an extremely long vision that I have been unable to recount the details with any clarity. All I can recall is that there was one point I was speaking with two spirits to my right. I was aware they were spirits and aware that I was in spirit form. They seemed startled when I asked them not to go anywhere – that I wanted to understand the situation better. Initially they

Rebirth I

faded out of my vision, but I asked them to come back. I could still hear their chatter. They came back for a bit and I asked them a lot of questions (of which I really did not receive any adequate answers). I felt they were unaware they existed in spirit form and not physical form, or perhaps they were surprised that I had as much clarity as I did regarding my awareness of my spiritual form. They seemed hesitant to help me understand anything further than I already knew in that moment.

Later in the vision I saw "the girl" briefly. She was observing my interactions. Some of the spirits continued to beg me to go party it up with them. I could tell the spirits with which I was interacting were not really aware of their own existence. It seemed almost as if it was in a place of limbo – where dreamers go, unaware they are dreaming. As I continually declined to go "party" and "drink" with the spirits, two female spirits came up and tried to sweet talk me into going with them. I told them specifically, "I cannot go." They, of course, asked why. I told them, "While I am aware I have stumbled in my earthly walk today, I am held to a higher set of standards and there is a line I cannot cross."

Confused, they continued to ask me what I was talking about and all I would repeat was "I have a higher set of standards to live up to. I am sorry, but I cannot go with you. Y'all have fun though!" All the while this conversation with the two female spirits occurred, "the girl" watched. As I stood firm in the struggle of temptation, she smiled. She smiled extremely big when the two spirits chose to let me be, and it was evident that I was holding strong to the spiritual standards that had been placed upon me.

Our eyes met and she knew that I saw her. She made no attempts to be hidden and was not subtle in the placement of her presence in that moment. I can only be sure that it was important for me to see her smile; to know that my earthly struggle during the day was not indicative of spiritual negligence and that my spirit held strong through the storm. It was also important that I recognized I was being watched – judged even – upon my actions and interactions. My earthly walk is an embodiment of my spiritual walk and I needed to understand my spirit's voice in the wake of earthly struggles. The standards to which I must live my earthly life have a higher bar set since I have been given the great gift of baptism in the spirit. All in all, that one smile said everything I needed to understand in that moment.

September 21, 2013

4:00 a.m.

I saw a tranquil place. A couple of others and I had just arrived at a location through the action of posing to be part of a train. We wandered around the place discussing how "we barely made it out of that one." There was a term we used for it, but I cannot remember it now. We moved into an older wooden building that reminded me of a western setting. Later, we wandered around. I was grabbed on the shoulder as we

Rebirth I

made our way to a set of tables that resembled card tables. These were being used for some form of testing which, apparently, I was about to experience. The person who grabbed my shoulder was my Indian spirit guide. I recognized him immediately. I have seen him before. He told the woman "not this one." And "not this time." She was puzzled and seemed frustrated that he interfered and spared me. I continued to observe the others.

My guide was very slick and was able to intervene without anyone noticing. He wanted me not to show I recognized him. Eventually as the group wandered around the veranda, we were told to introduce ourselves. We made our introductions as we walked about the setting. It was similar to a convention where everyone was checking out each booth. As we made our way to a group of musicians, I noticed my Indian friend was one of them. We introduced ourselves without names. The woman was watching over my shoulder – observing if I would give away that I knew him. After we exchanged welcomes, he slipped me a piece of paper with a word on it, as well as a folded brochure (to mask what he gave me). I knew it was important not to look then. I had a feeling I already knew the word, but he was trying to remind me of it.

I turned to go to the next booth and suddenly a deck of cards fanned beside my right eye. "Queen, seven, five? What did you see?" I was asked. I said, "What?" Surprised. The question was repeated. And she added, "Red, black, etc.". My Indian guide stepped in and said, "That's enough" to her. They were obviously having some conflicts about me. I said,

The Written

"Seventeen. Black... spades I think and perhaps a heart. Queen perhaps. I wasn't paying attention." She seemed judgmental but as if I had proven her right.

She said, "Interesting..." as she flashed the cards at me again more slowly. This time she revealed two black sevens and two red sixes. I said that I would try again. I had no idea what to expect, I told her that it was my fault for not being aware and that the burden was on me to prove myself. The Indian guy touched my shoulder and said "Water. Drink plenty of water." He then took a brief test in my place when it appeared. I told him I would prove him right for sticking up for me. He reiterated, "Water." I was told to move on, and we all moved back to the building. While there, the Indian found me again.

He said that I needed to align items in a certain part of the building. He said, "Trouble is coming and in order to protect others, you have to do it." I wasn't sure what "do it" meant, so I started trying to ask someone. A girl was moving stools around to a particular place in the building. She instructed me to help. As I began to help – unsure what to move – I passed by the Indian. I asked him again what I was doing. He replied angrily, "Shhhh! You are going to disrupt my vision from what happens next. You have to save them or the gunmen will kill everyone here. We need to place items that will distract them for a brawl (stools, etc.) so we can get everyone out."

We moved the stools around and put the women in a particular place in the room. Soon, a group of western robbers

Rebirth I

showed up. They acted as the guide said they would, attempting to hold up the building. We fought. I showed no fear around their guns and they seemed almost confused at my recklessness in the face of weapons. I stole or ripped apart most of the guns from their hands returning them one by one to my group. They seemed surprised too. Eventually there was one gunman left. I ran at him and grabbed his gun. It was firing (but making no sound) as we wrestled for it. Eventually I pointed it at his face where he was squirted with water. "Water, water. It is a water gun," I heard exclaimed. Suddenly his friend asked how many bullets he had left for his real gun. The guy replied, "Twenty-six." I immediately searched a box on the desk and found his gun – clip empty. I took it and returned it. The robbers yelled at each other and decided to leave.

The group of people I had ridden on the train with all seemed content we had completed the mission. We then went outside to try to smuggle our way onto the original train as a new train was pulling into the station. We began to sneak onboard, but had to be cautious because there were guards keeping watch. My vision ended before the train pulled out.

In another vision I was walking a dog and carrying a bowl of oatmeal. The bowl fell, and I stained two shirts. I could see two others across the way in the building. Somehow I, an acquaintance named J.T., and a former coworker named Andy were having a conversation about how I was owed damages for Andy's company having stained my shirts. Jason (a friend on earth) appeared. He had introduced me to Andy in the vision, but was timid once he knew the gravity of the situation.

The Written

In another vision, the setting was at night. There was a man with a miniature pet pig on his desk. The pig's feet were in a single jar (a third the size of its total body length). Apparently the jar was how he was teaching it to be obedient. I was entirely confused at everything surrounding the pig. It made no sense, but to the man I was talking about it with, the pig was an extremely good pet and well trained. Indeed the pig never moved. The vision ended with no resolve.

In reflecting upon the events, I wanted to make note that the Indian spirit guide has shown up multiple times, but I usually fail to remember the visions. He has definitely been a part of my journey and training. I did feel that he protected me from "failing" a test he knew I could pass under the right circumstances. The card game that I missed the answers to were relatively close enough to the real numbers that the girl became puzzled at how close I was when she wanted to dismiss me. She knew I saw red and black and also a seven (from the number seventeen, which isn't even a card number). But, overall, I feel that whatever tests I am poised to be completing on my astral journey, I am falling short of expectations to some members, where others (such as my guide) see potential.

October 9, 2013

Today during meditation, I witnessed a stack of items placed before me. From the dirt of the Earth to the top there was an oriental style rug spread across the dirt. On top of the

Rebirth I

rug was a thin white rectangular platform. The platform was probably only ½ an inch thick, but it stretched longer and wider than the rug. On top of the white rectangular platform was a cube – a pedestal approximately 2'x2'x2'. The rug seemed to represent the Earth. The white platform represented a bridge to the heavens. The cube represented the opportunity to bridge the boundaries of Earth to the Heavens and converse with God. As I stood on the platform, I found myself asking – pleading perhaps – into the light above longing for an answer to understand how to use the Lion of Judah within me. I have recently become more aware of its existence and I know it is beginning to let me know that I should learn how to harness it. As I asked, a voice rang out from the light, "You are not yet ready." I immediately became aware that the voice came from a looming figure before me that I could not visually identify, for the light was too bright for me to discern any features.

It was at this point the pedestal I was standing upon disappeared beneath my feet. The rectangular platform then disappeared fully exposing the rug below. At this point a giant footprint appeared on the rug. The footprint was glowing white and was the imprint of a left foot. As the footprint appeared I heard a rumble as if the world shook around me from the wake of the footstep.

The feelings I can describe in that moment were highlighted by submission, humility and inspiration. Obviously any conversation of this magnitude is humbling and inspiring, but I believe my pride has potentially impeded my spiritual walk.

This pride is what I believe was being highlighted from the voice through the demonstration of the footstep. While I am sure the footstep carries many meanings, the immediate feeling I felt was one of, "Here's the path. Get on it. Why did you step off of it? This isn't a game." I am paraphrasing, but I would be lying if I did not say I felt saddened that I am apparently not where I need to be in my spiritual walk in the eyes of the elders. I was not aware that I had allowed pride to creep in – and I do not know that I would have ever identified it as such, but that was the emotion I felt, so it must be the case….no questions asked. When the Lord tells you point-blank to "soldier up," those words are difficult to swallow. I cannot be entirely sure that was His intention in the words and vision, but I know that I felt I had been told a brutal truth about how I was still naïve in understanding. The coming days will be very important for me to reshape my direction as I will continue to search for resolve in my spiritual walk.

October 11, 2013

Bryan's projection as written by him to me in a text: "A box of keys, or a sledgehammer? Which gets you through faster? But what about Jonathan? He may not follow, yet be careful what you ask for! Walls with murals of Adam and Eve…She took the hammer, and ran through the door, perhaps on my unspoken request. Boston, "Let Me Take You Home Tonight" was playing on the phonograph….there I was,

Rebirth I

at Glenwood apartments, as a child...only, I, saw me...I hugged onto dad for dear life...even when she said let go, I refused....I may've really messed up. The walls of the corridors were painted with murals of the fall...it wasn't a curse; it was a consequence! Omni-benevolence never has an agenda. A loving God is never evil. You were there...yet separated by a wall. Pandora's Box and the Tree of Life are tantamount."

After receiving this text and before we spoke, I remembered a vague projection of congratulating him on being able to see his father and interact with him. I told Bryan while we were in the heavens, "That is amazing. I am so happy for you. Congratulations! Just – congratulations. That's awesome." It turns out, I was able to witness his projection in a way where we were each there in that moment, with different lenses to the situation of his father. I saw blackness, but saw Bryan. He saw me witnessing it, but knew I could not see through the wall – that part was only for him to see. All of this was confirmed in our conversation.

October 11, 2013

Last night in the heavens I was taught that liquid and solids are compressible. Gas is incompressible. This fact was continually reiterated to me over and over again. Though I repeated it back to the black man in a white robe, I felt like it was counterintuitive to what we know in western science. I think this is tied to my twenty-eight page paper on the compression of space/time I recently wrote but have yet to show anyone. Solids and liquids as being compressed matter makes sense. However, I felt like what I was being told was the opposite of logic because it seemed to state that what was already compressed was compressible. That which was uncompressed in our eyes is incompressible. Bryan seemed to think this was an explanation of matter on the other side of our reality.

October 12, 2013

Bryan's projection: "I traveled through a desert, on the back of a lion. We passed a wrecked ship and an evil person. I reached for my sword, and The Lion growled. The poem "Footprints", which once seemed trite, now made sense. If I had dismounted The Lion, I would've lost him forever. He carried me to a building filled with familiar faces. In the back, a boy (42yrs) sat in his father's lap. I looked out the window to see a storm. When I commented, the boy laughed and said, 'Storm? Ha! It's only started thundering, Talon.'"

October 13, 2013

4:08 a.m.

I had sense of touch, taste, smell, sight, sound – fully interactive and very lucid. A man greeted me. He asked me to follow him to the elevator. I knew he was my teacher and he introduced himself as such – but his introduction was not ver-

Rebirth I

bal, so I am summing up his intro. We spoke with words in every other aspect though.

He talked to me the whole time. We made small talk. I was very aware of the experience. The bellhop looked at me strangely. I high-fived him because I was so excited to see my guide. The guide looked like a mix of Colin from the comedy show with Drew Carey and the scraggly-haired Doc from the movie "Back to the Future." The bellhop seemed to think I was crazy. My guide told me to "chill out and calm down." I was asking a lot of questions, but not getting a lot of answers.

I saw a man in a suit and "blazer." He took me to a mezzanine. We walked by a kiosk/bar and he told me to wait there. I sat down. I talked to my "girlfriend" who was working at a cafe bar kiosk. She had long dark brown hair and brown eyes. She had the appearance of a girl next door.

As I sat down, he told me to wait there. She came over and asked me how I was doing. I was so ecstatic to interact with everyone. I asked her what my name was, then I said, "Better yet, what is the man's name who just left me here?" I was firing off questions in such a childlike manner. She looked at me oddly but carried on. I asked her what my name was again. She was curious why I would ask but was very "into me." She was clearly entertained by me.

I kept talking to her. I tried to explain I wanted to know my name, "Like my cousin Bryan was named Talon." She froze and said, "Stop it." She was freaked out as if she had seen a ghost. I said, "No, I am serious." She kept saying, "Stop it" like she could not believe what I was saying. I stopped, realizing I was speaking divinity before her and it suddenly appeared more real than myth.

I said, "You didn't see him did you?"

She said, "Who?"

I said, "The man who I came in here with."

She said, "You didn't come in with anyone.

I replied, "Sure I did."

Then I realized the gravity of it all. I said, "Ah, I get it. There are multiple dimensions here." She was confused. I continued on. "Like what is here and what you can't see. Right?" She still looked like she had seen a ghost and started fidgeting with stuff. I was puzzled. I said, "Seriously, what is my name?"

She said that she didn't think I was supposed to know that but she'd try to find out. She spoke those words shyly and quietly. That part confused me because it meant she was privy to the knowledge, but not the situation I was in. Also – the situation I was in was on a higher dimensional level than hers – so it seemed.

The man came back and wanted to see if I could follow him. He told me to stop talking to my girlfriend. I think he was being funny, but I wondered if she and I were in a relationship in some alternative universe.

I wandered around this bustling place with him while studying his face and clothes. They were similar to our clothes on Earth today. His clothes were navy. His jacket had a little plaid to it. His shirt had a mock collar.

Rebirth I

I started asking him about my name. I was very direct. I told him I was aware I was there and really needed to know. He laughed and said I did not need to know.

I said, "Yes I do. Like my cousin's name is Talon."

He stopped. His tone and demeanor changed into a more caring parental mode. He looked at me and said, "You know he's going through his own challenges right now." He seemed very serious about the gravity of it. I acknowledged. He said we would both be fine, but I didn't need my name yet. I asked his – he just laughed. This banter continued for what seemed like forever. It was all in good humor, and the situation felt like a training exercise.

I walked around with him for so long. Upstairs, I ate their food – a sloppy cheese-something that required fourteen napkins for me to stay clean. At one point, I grabbed a napkin from a buffet where lines of people were – like at a hotel convention food booth. The man gave me a fried mushroom creation. I asked other people if I was alone or with a man. Everyone said alone. He told me to follow him.

The world was created before me. I told him his suit looked nice. He said it was a "blazer." I kept talking to him as if he was there. He had to keep warning me not to because I'd look crazy to everyone. Sure enough I made several people uneasy, but I was okay with it because I knew what was around me.

He told me to wait. As he wandered off, I heard him say, "Let's see if you can find me." I instinctively headed toward his voice. Everything rescaled before me – grass, shrubbery, plants, etc. I eventually arrived where, upon my arrival, he said, "Good." He then wandered off to have me try something harder. As I walked around in search of him I became more aware of the absence of his presence and of my astral duality. I tried to fight it though – to stay in this place. Eventually I decided to wake up and write this down so I wouldn't forget. That was a hard decision.

October 13, 2013
11:00 a.m.

"The girl" appeared. She made me feel Loved with a kiss. After the kiss, I was taken to a football field. I was playing football with a guy that resembled Peyton Manning and one other receiver. We'd continue to run routes, but the ball was thrown so hard it always went through my hands (off my fingertips). I kept being told to try again. Every time, the ball was hurled so fast it would go off the tips of my fingers. I took this to mean I am starting to get practice reps on the football field with the big kids. (No longer on the playground) But – I am also not ready.

October 14, 2013

I was in a store – much like a Wal-Mart or Target, but much bigger. I was with "the girl." On instruction, I left her in the front of the store as I walked back to the music section. I

Rebirth I

looked for Kip Moore's albums. I found several albums of his (in reality he only has one at present) and eventually my eyes fell on a larger box – reminiscent of older box sets of CDs. I picked it up. It was brown and tan. On the cover was Kip's name and picture…clearly a boxed set of his. Along the bottom of the box was a list of 5 names. These names were a list of people who helped shape his life. There was also an anomaly in the list: the first line which said in bold, "The _____ Cellis." The blank was another descriptive word that I thought illustrated "saddest" to describe the celli word, but I could not distinguish it. Possibly, the first line was a reference to a person – a spiritual elder. That is what my impression was, but I also tied the name to the musical instrument – the cello – and the significance of the sound it produces. I was left to assume that he found significance in the sound of multiple cellos – or one in particular that was worthy of listing on the cover of this box.

As I studied the box, I had recognition that this was Kip's effort to say thanks. I recognized that he made a special effort to make sure everyone knew he was – and would always be – thankful for the efforts people made to help shape his career. The other recognizable name on the box was the very bottom name: "John Wayne and Andrea Armour." John Wayne is who originally introduced Kip and me before he moved to Nashville. Rightly so, John Wayne would be on the cover as well as the bookend to the list since he single handedly helped Kip get a demo from me which he would go on to use in pitching himself as an artist in Nashville.

The Written

I carried the box up to the front to show "the girl." I knew it was important – and it was also the item I was supposed to find. As I carried it up, I recognized that there was an old cassette strapped to the box indicating it was an older box set. I was very confused, and this brought me to the recognition that I was not on Earth. I went back and found a box set that did not have a cassette attached. I returned to the front where the girl smiled and was glad I had found the box. She then asked me to follow her around, of which I obliged her, and the world dissipated.

After reflecting on the experience, I realized it was important for me to know that I really did help shape Kip's life – as did John Wayne. Whether I am to ever receive recognition of it from Kip, I know he is genuinely thankful and the angels felt that I deserved to know it. It was like the Heavens were tying up loose ends for me. These loose ends were answers to questions I continually wonder about in different parts of my life – such as what was, what could've been, what would've been, what should've been. I've wondered if I was supposed to have some role in the music industry if my life had taken another path. But in this moment, I realized that none of the potential mattered, only what actually occurred. And – the events that did occur were all that was supposed to have happened all along. So, my thoughts should be viewed as just wasted effort in that space. I should know that I served the purpose – a purpose that was to be – a call that I answered. And in this, I had peace.

Rebirth I

October 14, 2013

A message I sent to my ex-brother in-law this morning

Hey – hope all is well with you. Last night I was shown a vision that I thought you should know about. I could describe in detail the circumstances and the events that led me to this understanding – but it is probably too long to write. Ultimately, yours and Andrea's name was on a list of 5 names that was shown to me by an angel to bring understanding to the circumstances of Kip's life. Yours and Andrea's name was on one line together: "John Wayne & Andrea Armour." It was the last line of the 5 names. It represented the bookend to the first name. I was in the middle of the list. It essentially meant that Kip would not be where he was today if it were not for the 5 people on the list. The first name on the list was a spiritual name (his Divine helper's embodiment). The other 4 lines were a list of people here on Earth. Your name being last represented the beginning and the end. If it were not for your chance encounter and interaction with him – then bringing him over to my place to record that day, he would not have gotten to where he is today. The list was also supposed to illustrate the 5 people that he is (and will always be) thankful for having entered into his life (whether he is ever able to communicate that to those that were on the list). It was important I was shown this list and there was much more to the vision than the list alone. But, I feel like it is important you know about the gravity of the role you played in his life and I hope that it provides perspective on the roles we play in our daily interactions with others. It is not about what we get out of it, but how we help shape others. This vision was to illustrate closure to questions unanswered. What would have happened if we kept writing for him? What would have happened if we didn't move our separate ways? etc. In the end, what hap-

pened was supposed to happen and the roles we played were the way it was intended. But there was a divine acknowledgement of the significance in helping others and our roles in that aspect of our walks through life. Anyway, hope you and Andrea are doing well. I hope this vision adds a bit of light to your day.

Jonathan

October 15, 2013

Bryan shared with me a voice he heard during his meditation today. "In defiance and contrary to the modalities of algorithmic logic, the firebrand is held by the hand of subservience and servitude."

October 17, 2013

Bryan shared with me potentially the biggest vision he has ever had. On this day I realized I was not just sharing conversation with another human being learning to grow in the spirit as I am. But instead, I am talking to an angel discovering who he is while in human form. And maybe – that is the case with me as well.

Bryan's vision began with him standing in a great hall. Along either side of him were two walls painted with giant murals. The murals seemed to depict the Garden of Eden with Adam and Eve, but Bryan was unable to study the walls too

Rebirth I

closely. Before him stood "The Girl." From this point forward, Bryan explained that everything he experienced was not in spoken word, but in intention. Bryan experienced, again, the flower of life, but this time it was illustrated in a different fashion. The girl showed him a line. She asked him what a line squared was. The answer was a square. She asked him what a square squared was. The answer was a cube. As she was asking the questions, the shape was formed in front of them. The cube revealed a circle nested precisely within each outer wall boundary. She then proceeded to push the bottom left corner of the square diagonally through to the top right corner on the back wall. As she performed this action, the walls of the cube folded in upon themselves so as to form a double walled version of the half-outer shell of a cube. From this point, a ball fell out of the square. She pulled her finger back out and the square reformed again. She repeated the action continually allowing a ball to fall out each time she revealed the shape within.

This vision stemmed some of the longest conversations Bryan and I have ever had. We discussed the significance of all that is, all that will be, and all that was: the infinite Is. We discussed the flower of life and how it mathematically forms the structure of the great infinite. Essentially every known (and misunderstood) principle in physics and geometry melded into one grand denouement of understanding. The knowledge of what Bryan and I have written in the past and most importantly the unwritten, answers the most fundamentally important questions that have plagued mankind for ages. Our discussions even led us to understand just how Jesus was able to manifest fish for thousands from the basket that held just a couple fish. While, this particular document is not the right place for a detailed exploration of the greatness that was revealed to Bryan, it was revealed to me by Bryan that he was to share this information with me so that I may bring its understanding to the masses.

October 18, 2013

Bryan shared with me the vision he had early this morning. He was standing in the middle of a great hall. On either side of him was a mural (the same one as in his previous vision). This time, he wanted to soak in the details of where he was. Each mural depicted a scene from the Garden of Eden with Adam and Eve. The mural showcased the Tree of Knowledge and how it transformed the perspectives of Adam and Eve once they partook in the forbidden fruit. Bryan shared with me how and why God allowed the events to unfold. His perspective was new – one that could only have been ascertained through the transformation we have been experiencing. Ultimately, the discussion led to a discourse on good versus evil and whether the Tree of Knowledge was truly good or evil.

The interesting part of this vision is that this morning I felt compelled to reread Genesis – something I had not done in at least five years – possibly ten years or more. I reread it una-

Rebirth I

ware of the vision Bryan was to share with me later that evening. And, in addition to wanting to reread Genesis, last night I watched "The Fountain" – an art-house movie centered around Buddhist beliefs on the Tree of Knowledge. Again, this was not a movie I had ever seen, but one I felt compelled to buy and watch after I noticed the universe nudging me that way. I had not shared with Bryan anything about the movie nor my intentions to even watch it. For all intents and purposes, Bryan and I had not once discussed anything pertaining to the movie at all.

So, armed with the new perspective from "The Fountain" and my new lens of understanding of the story in Genesis, the discussion with Bryan about his vision was much more academic than it would have been otherwise. I was able to offer fresh perspective as Bryan shared his. It turned out to be a very engaging conversation.

But Bryan's vision did not end with him standing in the great hall with the murals. He proceeded to open the door at the end of the hall. This door was the same one the angel broke through with the sledgehammer in his previous vision. When he entered, there were two entities standing before him. They were formless – without definition. They asked Bryan if he knew where he was. Bryan replied that he did not know. They warned Bryan that it may be difficult for him to see what he was about to see if he did not know where he was, but Bryan was determined to see the demonstration. He was directed to look around him. He looked all around the room at the whitest of light – the whitest of walls. He knew he was standing

The Written

inside of a sphere, but unsure of how big the sphere was. The formless girl, walked into the middle and reached her hands up causing the sphere to begin scaling down upon itself. Bryan was forced to the outside of the sphere he was standing within, but was now encompassed within another sphere. Essentially a second sphere closed around the first sphere as the first sphere contracted. Bryan described himself as feeling breathless – in a void, but only outside of the immediate sphere. He recognized he was still somewhere important, but at that moment he lost his bearings and lost the vision.

When Bryan described this to me, I knew immediately what he had seen. I asked if he knew what a tesseract was. Bryan said he knew the word, but could not describe it nor had he ever seen an animation of one. I directed him to an animation of a cube expanding and compressing upon itself. The tesseract is the best attempt that a wireframe animation can do in describing a fourth dimension. But, as we had discussed from his previous vision, there is no such thing as a line. Therefore, the tesseract animation now had new meaning. If a person is to visualize spheres bound within the cubes of the animation, the experience would be as Bryan described. Bryan was blown away. He admitted that it was indeed the experience he had, but would never even have been able to relate it to the tesseract animation had the previous vision not occurred.

Rebirth I

October 18, 2013

I was in a room. Everything about the environment felt dirty…filthy…grimy. A man stood in front of a naked woman on a bed. He was dark and sinister, yet his appearance was cordial and inviting. The feelings I had caused me to feel as if I was literally seeing the filth even though appearances were not as I described. The man stepped away from the girl. She was on her back – legs open for me. She was very attractive, her eyes inviting – perhaps even beautiful. But, she too exuded the same feelings that marred my vision of the man and the room. The only thing I could rationalize in the moment was that she was filthy and dirty. The man introduced us and made small talk to make me more comfortable in the moment. The girl rolled over on her forearms and knees. She opened her legs wider for me and pushed her chest into the bed, causing her rear to be forced up and onto me. The man nudged me into her, telling me to go ahead and do whatever I desired. I knew in that moment that I could do whatever my flesh desired to the girl and she would fulfill my every want and dream. But, I couldn't. Inside of me, I had the true recognition of what I was experiencing. Perhaps if I had not been forced into the girl by the hand of Evil, I would not have recognized it as easily. But the sensation that went through my body as I was nudged was one that I would never hope to feel again. The feeling of chill – a dark, sinister and foreboding feeling – rushed through to my core. On a dime, I immediately stopped my carnal desires.

The Written

I said, "I can't. I just can't." The man was confused and asked why. I repeated, "I can't. It's not right." As I turned to walk away, I heard "The Girl" say, "Good" and then I awoke.

The girl's voice at the end was a small acknowledgement that I correctly discerned the forces of good and evil. It was not that sex was evil – far from it. Sex is a beautiful act our bodies and spirits are meant to experience. But it can also be the greatest temptation. So, for me to have evil masked through the experience of unlimited carnal desires with a beautiful woman – and for me to have the willpower and recognition to resist evil's presence in that moment – was a major win through the lessons of the spiritual battlefield. I'm thankful "The Girl" was there to witness it. Or, perhaps I would not have been there if she had not invited me into that moment where she was observing my growth in the spirit. Either way, this was a lesson similar to Bryan's journey on the back of the Lion and seeing evil in the distance.

October 20, 2013

Tonight I saw "the girl" twice. She was standing in the distance walking toward me. Each time I did not realize it was her – I only realized it after each time she passed by. Nothing came of it, but I am sure that she was waiting for me to recognize her so we could continue on our lessons.

Rebirth I

October 26, 2013

I was standing before "the girl." She asked me to get into a vehicle and drive. I had a few drinks the evening before and since I am very cognizant of making sure I do not drink and drive, I told her I would not. She continued to press me to drive. I held my ground. Eventually I got into the vehicle with her in the passenger seat. She told me not to worry – that I would not get in trouble for drinking and driving. She told me that I was fine. As I began to drive, I could tell the steering was difficult. She asked me to drive down a grassy hill. On the right side of the open grassy area was some sort of a concrete median with a fountain. As I coasted down the hill, I bounced onto the median and back into my lane. When we reached the bottom, we were in the parking lot of a larger building. It looked like a roundabout in front of a fancy hotel. I jumped out of the vehicle and told her "Never again." I was adamant that I would never drive after drinking, but she continued to tell me that everything was okay and that I could drive. My heart raced – panicked as if I was about to experience the wrath of a judicial system coming down on me.

As we stood there, a man came out of the building and told me we could not park where the vehicle had ended up. He told me to move it one parking place over. I would not do it. I held strong to my moral compass. I decided to walk away from them. I had the feeling as if I was walking home. I walked up the hill, crossed the street, and turned East. I

The Written

walked in that direction for a mile or two. I walked through the remnants of a party scene littered across the front yards of several houses in a row. I continued past them.

The sun was rising. I finally arrived at what I thought was my house. I walked inside, relieved to have made it home after that experience. But, to my surprise, the house was full of people. They all looked at me oddly. I asked them what they were doing at my house – that I was supposed to be alone and go to bed. They all told me they thought the same thing, but everyone ended up here with the same type of confusion. I decided to walk back from where I came. I left the house (a two story concrete block style house). I walked back through the remnants of the party scenes kicking an empty beer can and whatever else I found in my way. I returned to the front of the building where "the girl" and the man from the building stood. I decided I would move the car for them. I backed the car into the parking spot one place over. They thanked me for doing that, but I replied that I was unhappy that they made me do it. I explained that I would not allow myself to get in trouble with the cops over this. It was easily preventable, etc. "The girl" looked at me again and told me that everything was fine and that nothing was going to happen. She continued to reassure me that I was in a safe place and that "nothing would happen."

After talking with Bryan about the vision later in the evening, he immediately realized a significance I did not see. I assumed that the message had to do with a black and white line on drinking and the spiritual walk – a conversation that

Rebirth I

Bryan and I have often. But Bryan offered up an amazing interpretation. He said that he immediately recognized that "the girl" was trying to get me to see the divide between empirical data and the ethereal experience. The fact that I had a few drinks the evening prior was empirical, yet I still found myself standing before the divine girl. It should have been obvious that I was still able to get to this place, and have experiences in the Heavens with this angel.

Bryan thought that the girl was trying to get me to recognize the divide. My mind felt the gravity of the earthly experience and was attempting to apply that empirical data to an experience where empirical data did not matter. Bryan thought "the girl" forcing me to drive the car was her showing me that I had to let go of the earthly mind for the full experience of the Heavenly plane. Bryan then pointed me to a song "Jerk it out" by the Caesars. Often messages are conveyed to Bryan and me through imagery and this case was no different. He said that while I was explaining my experience that he was impressed with the chorus to the song – which we went on to analyze as expressing the spirit within and pulling it out and into the world.

After our conversation ended, I decided to watch the music video to see if there was an additional message. Sure enough, while most of the video is of the band playing the song on a stage, the chorus cuts to them driving a car down the road while partying – and pouring out some type of drink from the window of the car. While this may not seem that big of a deal to others, for me it was confirmation that Bryan's interpretation was correct. That not only had he shared with me the proper analysis, but the lyrics to the song were applicable. And, by watching the video and witnessing my experience occur during the chorus of the song was pretty much a divine confirmation. I texted Bryan and as it turns out, he had no recollection of the video – only the song from fifteen to twenty years ago. He only knew that the song came into his head while I was sharing my story, thus adding credence to a divine interpretation (not that I had doubts anyway – I put this in for the reader to understand how these things work; subtle yet grandiose).

October 27, 2013

Bryan shared with me a vision he experienced during the early morning. He awoke at 4:00 a.m. having experienced the type of vision where one would question whether it was reality or a dream. He was in Heaven surrounded by a lot of people moving in the same direction. He knew there was some type of wedding or ceremony that everyone was making their way to attend. Suddenly, a guy (slender in build, but well cut and defined) slapped him on the shoulder. With no words, the word "Akros" was impressed upon Bryan. At the time, he assumed the guy was introducing himself, but later, thoughts on the experience opened the potential for other meanings.

So, as they stood together, Akros looked at Bryan and asked if he was ready. Bryan said he was. Akros asked if he

Rebirth I

could keep up. Bryan, unsure of the moment ahead, said he could and that he was ready. They ran. They ran all around the heavens in ways similar to the experiences that Bryan has had with "the girl." Akros led Bryan into the wedding ceremony. Standing in a great opening of tiered verandas, stood angels – all similar in form. They stood with the same postures. They were iconic in stature and form. Each of their heads tilted at the same precise angle. Their faces were comprised of three animals: the face of a baboon, the head of an eagle, and an owl. Their bodies were divine – angelic with wings. Bryan had the impression they were angelic warriors.

Akros led Bryan into a veranda and told him not to worry – that the angels would not notice him. While none of the angels changed their stature, Bryan did feel there was one angel who stared him down as if to say, "This is important. Do NOT act up." The ceremony proceeded. While Bryan never saw the events of the ceremony (he had no line of sight to the event itself), he did see a girl walk by with a bold, blue sky behind her. He thought it was "the girl" but she was in another form.

After the ceremony, Akros asked Bryan if he was ready to keep up with him. Bryan obliged. Akros ran quickly over to a green path that led up a wall. Akros had defied our earthly concept of gravity and was now standing with his feet on the path, but parallel to the ground below. Bryan followed. When he caught up, Akros told him to "hang in there" as they both dashed down the hill faster than ever before. Bryan and Akros ran side-by-side laughing and enjoying the moment. At the

The Written

end of the path, they came to a door. Akros opened it up to reveal that it was raining on the other side. Akros ran out into the rain. As Bryan followed, he heard Akros say "Don't...." and in that moment, Bryan awoke.

Bryan felt like Akros was about to tell him, "Don't let the rain affect your focus" but the sensation was too much for Bryan to handle, and it caused him to awaken. Bryan told me how he recognized a message in duality — that throughout the entire experience, there was a theme of two-as-one. When Akros and Bryan ran, they were side-by-side, step-in-step. They were acting as one, but for them to do what they experienced, they had to align themselves so as to be one. Additionally, the ceremony was indicating that two were becoming one. It was an important ceremony in the Heavens that he was privileged to witness and experience.

In our discussion, Bryan and I discussed the word Akros and the message that was passed on to him. Bryan felt there was an extreme significance in the duality he experienced and the importance of the duality in our spiritual walks together. The message echoed the importance of each of us having to work as one to achieve the goal. We discussed references in the Bible of the pairs of people – Elisha and Elijah, etc.

Near the end of our conversation, we chatted about the significance of the word Akros. While at the time of the experience, Bryan felt that the name of the guy he was running around the Heavens with was Akros, there is a possibility that the angel passed Bryan on my name. We will not know for sometime, but I will ask my guardian at a point down the road

Rebirth I

if my name is Akros. Maybe he will oblige and tell me – or maybe I will have to remain without a name for a while. But, the possibility exists that Bryan was imparted my name. Perhaps it was a higher spiritual self of me. Perhaps it was another angelic being named Akros. There have been so many questions raised within each of our experiences, that it does not do a lot of good to attempt to place an empirical rationalization upon them. At this point, each experience is to be added to the knowledge bank so that one day all of the pieces will form a greater understanding of the puzzle we are experiencing.

October 29, 2013

Today I had lunch with Julie – a friend that I have not seen in a couple of years. During the hardest points in my life, we always found ourselves hanging out late at night talking about all of the challenges of the world: what we were meant for, what roles we were playing at that moment, the great divide in where we felt led versus where we were in the present. She began to figure it out before me and in that time we went our separate ways. She went in the direction her spiritual growth led her. I continued to find myself further and further in the darkness. But today, our lives had transcended the plane from before. She has become such a beautiful woman inside and out. She leaves for an 11 month mission trip in a couple of months and I can't help but feel her excitement. It is like watching a plane depart in all of its majestic wonder. I can't

The Written

help but wonder where her life is leading – but I already know the destination. I guess the thought of seeing her life blossom from the window has captured my curiosity. And perhaps there is a little jealousy – though not in an ego kind of way – more like anticipation in my own walk. I can't wait to experience the greater plans my Father has for me – and I do wrestle with that very thought every day. The truth is that I should embrace the moment…this second….the present. Everything else is immaterial and serves no purpose other than to distract me from my present course. At the very least I acknowledge it. But in that acknowledgement, I am still hanging onto something I shouldn't – and therein lies my greatest challenge.

I've known for the last several days that I have been struggling with this step of my journey. It has not been a struggle of who I am, but of who I will become. My focus has been locked on the future – and in that tunnel vision I have lost track of the present. During lunch I found myself sitting on the opposite side of the table where I normally take others who are seeking insight from my growth — those who have reached out because they have noticed our great Creator flowing through me. It isn't really anything they have said that has allowed me to notice, but instead it has been in what their spirit said that called attention to mine. In that acknowledgement of spiritual conversation, a greater discernment of the moment takes place. So, to find myself in the seat of those seeking something greater was somewhat ironic – though perfectly in synchrony in the present. For, it was I who needed help – and would receive help and perspective in our conversation. And

Rebirth I

truth be told, I will always find myself in this seat, for so is the way our journey through the human experience occurs.

During our conversation, I wanted to learn about Julie's upcoming mission trip. Instead, through listening to her speak, I managed to hear a greater message. I came to realize that the obstacle impeding the next step of my journey was not ego – but rather that somehow I have watered the seed of ego and allowed it to take root in my being. I pondered how I was to cut off the supply of the seed's nutrients….a question that I did not have an answer for. But then the realization came that perhaps it was not an action that I needed to figure out how to do, but rather an inaction that should take place in order to cut off the supply of nutrients. "Cutting off" was more analogous to "not feeding" than an actionable item. It was like the definition of darkness, which is "the absence of light." One cannot exist without the removal of one from the other.

This is the first time I have experienced this much awareness of an overabundance of ego in my life. Perhaps it isn't a larger portion of ego that is noticeable in my life, but rather a greater awareness to the ego that was already present. Over the last several days, I was viewing this awareness of ego like an annoying gnat that kept flying into my face – a problem that I thought I could easily swat away. But the reality is that the gnat is more like a netting that has encumbered me – and the more I struggle to swat it away, the more deeply caught up in it I will become.

As Julie and I parted ways, I prayed aloud on my drive back to the office about the revelations in that moment. I ram-

The Written

bled on, stream-of-consciousness style to my Creator. I am sure that God has a sense of humor because I would have laughed at myself if I had to listen to my offered up conversation and the eventual epiphany that occurred in the end. But the epiphany did not come during the conversation. The epiphany came through the questions that remained open-ended as I parked and headed toward the parking garage stairwell outside of my office.

Getting out of my Jeep and walking toward the stairwell, my hand came to rest next to a ladybug on the door handle. A simple sign that has occurred throughout the course of my journey, said so much in its own way – affirmation to my earlier conversation and introspection. And upon walking toward the front door of my office building, I heard crickets – the sound of that spiritual chorus of recognition. The third moment came upon entering the building and passing by the food stand in our lobby. The owner – a jovial man who always takes the time to greet me by name – managed to answer my atypical question about his day before I even finished asking the question. In fact, he stopped answering half way through when he recognized that he was answering my thought – and not my completed question. So between the ladybug, the crickets, and the interconnected conversation in the lobby, I knew that the question with which I had closed up my conversation with God was being answered in such a subtle, but grandiose way. I heard His voice trough everything around me: "You are on the right path. Just keep moving forward.

Rebirth I

Don't pause to figure it out, but figure it out through the motion of the direction forward."

October 30, 2013

This morning I arrived at work feeling compelled to write. I found that my username to log onto my computer had expired. I have practiced in IT for 15 professional years and to have a username expire is one of the most atypical problems to have in the way the IT infrastructure operates. I instinctively saw the conversation taking place. I texted Bryan to tell him how the events of the day would play out. I am on a long term contract with this client so my login credentials had been setup in an open fashion. The only possible reason that my credentials would have expired was if I had been intentionally shut out of the system: as if my contract was terminated and this was the way I would discover it as such. I asked the VP that I reported to if anything had changed with my contract – I was assured, "most definitely not." To even reinforce this, at the end of the day I was called into his office to discuss coming on board full time. Having (thought I had) understood the message from earlier, I figured this was a point on my journey to determine whether I would move onto the next thing God has planned in my life.

When I discussed the events with Bryan, he immediately recognized a greater message in his interpretation. He felt that the events of today were God's way of saying, "Hey – I tried to see how you handled driving the car when I visited you in your dreams before. Today, I am going to see how you handle placing faith in me throughout your day." And what a wise interpretation it was. Indeed, I had placed my confidence in God and had found peace in whatever direction the day's events would take me. It wasn't about the future, but about the present and not being disrupted in my confidence with my walk with God.

November 1, 2013

"Head up. Angel up. It is important today." These were the words that were imparted to me as I awoke today. Bryan also awoke with knowledge he had been imparted in the night. He suddenly understood the meaning of the book of Job. The three battles of Sachin Kata were encoded within the book of Job. "What you are versus who you are" was an important theme today.

November 2, 2013

My vision lasted the duration of several days. In the beginning, I was having dinner and met a father separated from his son approximately seventeen years prior. All he could do was tell me how much he Loved him and did not know how to find him. He was confident that his son did not even know who he was or how to find him. His dad left me a business

Rebirth I

card – but not because he was asking me to help. The business card was just a formality of introductions between each of us. The first name that he continued to tell me was something along the lines of "Uninana-(qua? Or el?)" though I didn't think it was his name, or his son's name. The name left me baffled more than anything. But the conversation broke my heart.

The next day in a conference room at work, I found myself talking to a young employee. He told me about his family and I knew instantly he was the son of the father. They even shared the same last name. I asked him more questions about his childhood. Eventually I told him I knew his father. He didn't believe be. I told him I had the man's card and shared with him the story of how I met his father. The next day I took the boy his card and he called his father. I told him that he could see for himself, and that I was merely a messenger in what I witnessed. I was amazed that I had been the glue to help the two find each other. I told everyone I knew about how the events unfolded. I had several people over to my house during the course of the next several days and shared with each of them the story. They seemed less blown away than I was. I told random people I struck up conversations with during dinners about the event. They were intrigued, but less understanding of the gravity of it.

On a less important note, we also discussed the restaurant above my condo unit and the restaurant below it. The building was similar to where I live today, but more developed. I have had other visions in this same place before – it is almost as if another location is specifically used for my spiritual experience. Also important in reflection was the place above represented a new location that I was welcomed into. Upon uniting the Father with the Son, I now convened in harmony with a group of other angels in their house above, instead of the house below. I was now able to experience the house above.

November 5, 2013

I awoke from a vision that was again illustrated through an earthly experience. I was guided by "the girl." She was with me throughout the whole experience. I managed to experience a full day of context during the brief vision. Though it is still hazy, I know that I experienced the following: I had to prepare a presentation for an employer. I seemed to dismiss the earthly significance and instead tried to take care of other priorities. I left work during lunch (with "the girl") and made several trips around an older town. I first went to my house where I spoke with my earthly father. I told him I was running late, but everything was going to be okay. I then drove "the girl" to another stop on my errands, which was to get some clothes fitted at an alterations place. When we parked, we got out and realized the shop was closed. We got back in the vehicle where I returned to work.

I remember being extremely stressed out because I had not accomplished much during that time. In fact, I was even a

Rebirth I

few minutes late for the presentation I had to make. We all sat around a conference room table. My father was present, as was an older gentleman with gray hair. My father spoke first – telling me I had my priorities all wrong and that I needed to focus on what was important. I became upset. I told him that everything was just fine – that he didn't see how I was able to still address the priorities of employment in such an efficient way. He became angry and told me that I was wrong and being ignorant. The older gentleman who I thought was an angel decided to chime in. I felt like he was my friend and was going to support me in my decisions, but he caught me off-guard. He bellowed his support of my father's words and told me I was being ignorant. He was visibly angry and I felt crushed that he did not support me either. I became upset and told them I had to excuse myself for a few minutes. I left and rushed to my desk where I wanted to quickly prepare my presentation for the head leader that was still not present in the room. I knew I had a few minutes and hoped that I could put it together quickly enough.

 I opened up Keynote and began to look at an older presentation that I was going to use to cobble together the presentation for that day. I scanned through it but there were so many words on each slide that I could not read them. I realized that words clouded the intention and missed the purpose of my presentation. I finally clicked through to a slide that had a video – The Spirit Molecule's video I had watched early in the day (in real life). The video was condensed and only consisted of the portion that discussed the flower of life. It finished

The Written

playing and the next several slides flowed beautifully together after it. I knew that everything else was unimportant in the presentation except for these slides. I also did not understand the purpose of the slides that were beautifully put together since they were unrelated to what I thought I was presenting, but I deleted everything else except for those slides.

    I walked back up to the room where more elders had gathered. I managed to make it in just prior to the leader entering the room. When it came my time to present, I explained that what the leader was about to see was important, but not what he was expecting to see. I told him that even though it may seem disconnected from his expectations, I could assure him that it was more intertwined than he realized. And with that, I started the first video with the flower of life. I turned to my father and the gray haired angel and said, "See – I told you I pick it up quickly. Just have some faith in me and trust me." At this moment I knew that I had completed the objective, though the journey was unmistakably inefficient and lacked the discipline in walk that the elders desired from me. I think I also demonstrated an arrogance that was unbecoming, but the arrogance was only in the confidence that I would succeed. In retrospect I was not happy with the way I handled the situation, but then again I also did not have any understanding of expectations, rules, etc. I see now that I acted like a child going through puberty – where I would complete tasks, but in my own way. I assume this is indicative of some amount of ego that is still tied to my spirit – the portion that I need to contin-

Rebirth I

ue to work on separating completely from my spirit. The vision ended in clarity at this point, but the vision did not end.

I found myself in a flux-like location where "the girl" was present, but shapes were no longer distinguishable. We discussed at length the comparisons I was drawing between the Hebrew alphabet, the 7 loci of communication, the trigrams in I-Ching, and the grid of Hebrew characters into mind, body and spirit. I was reassured that I was on the right path. Though I was not shared any additional information, upon asking, she assured me that I needed to continue down this path and that I was correct at the conclusions I had arrived at so far. All I could understand was that I was on the cusp of unlocking very important knowledge that holds a greater key within. I longed to know more, but was intentionally not shared more information in order to help my growth.

I awoke assured in my progress, the importance of this part of my journey, and motivated to continue my research into the subject. Of note regarding my feelings on the meeting I had been involved in during the earlier part of the projection – in my waking moments I felt shame in my approach to completing the mission, embarrassing arrogance in being nonchalant, stressed from the experience but with understanding that the stress was due to my personal fault, disappointment in upsetting the elder and my father, but a sense of success in completing the mission through the methods, message and conclusions I went on to present to the leader. Overall, I'd say it was a disappointing feeling – one that was of re-experiencing a self-indulged and prideful journey of a person with so much potential, who was blindly missing the understanding of how to handle the potential. And therein is one of the many lessons of my vision.

November 5, 2013

Today I met with Dan to discuss the book he sent me a few weeks ago. The book was A New Earth by Eckhart Tolle. As we sat down to discuss the book, I shared with him how I read the book at a time in my journey when I really needed to hear those words. I explained how I had been having difficulty breaking free of my ego during the days prior to reading the book. When I picked up the book, I managed to read it nearly straight through.

We went on to talk about some of the challenges he was facing – stress from planning for his financial future seemed to be the subject plaguing his mind the most. I shared with him parts of my journey that had led me to deal with those same challenges head on. I quoted many parts of the book we were discussing – not intentionally – but because the words held within them the answers he was seeking. The book had not just been a message for me, but a message for Dan that I could interpret for him. We also spent time discussing how God speaks to each of us.

I shared with him how God communicates in three ways: (1) through daily interactions/environment, (2) through the voice of another person, and finally (3) through the visions of

Rebirth I

the night. Dan told me how he was unable to dream and that he had tried for so long to dream. I shared with him that which I have learned: the visions of the night are accessible by all, but only to those who have cried out for help along the journey and whom He has shown favor. And, perhaps favor would better be described as acknowledgement of a humbled person open to the acceptance of His Word.

After we parted ways I sent him the handful of lines that I found most important for me during reading. As it would turn out, he had highlighted the same lines during his initial read from a few years prior. The first verse I sent him and the last verse I had highlighted dealt specifically with anxiety – the very subject he discussed with me the most.

November 6, 2013

This morning I received a text from Dan letting me know that he had experienced a dream for the first time that he could ever remember and was able to write it down. Praise be to God for He heard and answered the call of Dan's humble desire to follow the light. He then blessed Dan with the visions of the night.

November 7, 2013

I was standing before a girl. The surroundings were hazy, but her face was the center of my attention and very much in

The Written

focus. She was beautiful, but in an earthly sense – not in the overpowering beauty of an angel. No words were spoken as she acknowledged my presence – just a slight nod of her head and a smile. Her eyes were warm and welcoming. Her hair was blonde with natural curls. I introduced myself as if this were the first time we had met. As the words rolled out of my mouth, I realized I was not experiencing a reality on Earth – I realized I was standing in the heavens and "the girl" before me was in earthly disguise. As I finished my introduction, my body filled with excitement and awareness of the moment. I looked deep into her eyes and said, "I know where I am. I also know that you are her in disguise." She smiled. An overwhelming, rushing feeling overtook my body and I was in the void.

I called out for her to wait for me as I focused on not losing the mindset to remain in the heavens. I knew that the experience was more than the yoke of my mind and spirit could contain. I focused and found calm in the moment. The heavens opened up before me and I was standing before "the girl." This time, she was in angelic form – beautiful, wearing a long, flowing green gown. She was taller than I – or perhaps I was shorter than she. If I identified myself as my earthly height of six feet tall, she was at least seven feet in height. But, her appearance was not intimidating. She looked down into my eyes and nodded her head in acknowledgement of my presence.

While the communication seemed to occur in thought and not words, the way we communicated felt as fluid as words being shared. However, there was no sound as she

Rebirth I

spoke. She said, "Follow me." We walked down a hallway and through a great door. We were standing in a library. She shut the door behind me. The last time I was in this same location I was overcome with questions and desire to ask my identity. The last time, I continued to ask, "Who am I?" It was the only question I wanted answered. But, from the last time until today I have learned that who I am is not important — nor is it the question I should ask. I understood the only questions surrounding my identity should be, "What am I?" and, "Where am I?"

I felt shame for the way I had behaved before. All of these thoughts struck me in one moment. As the door shut, I took a few steps, turned to my left, and stood before a great wall of books. The shelving was made of a highly polished cherry/walnut wood. The shelving was in and of itself a meticulously crafted design. The girl passed behind me and stood to my right, the door that we had entered was on my left. Everything was so vivid. I placed my hands in front of my abdomen, fingertips touching fingertips as if in contemplation. The girl began to search for a book. I was humbled to have been welcomed back into this room again. I looked over at the girl and said, "Before we go any further, I have to let you know how sorry I am for my actions from the last time I was here. I know just to be here is a blessing and the last time all I wanted to do was ask for my identity — which was my ego speaking. I missed the greater message. Now I know that the question I should have asked was not 'who am I', but rather 'what am I' or 'where am I' — but honestly, none of that matters to me anymore. I am perfectly okay with not knowing because I do not need to know."

She nodded – a slight acknowledgement to let me know that it was okay because I recognized my wrongs and that I still am progressing on the right path – but also, to acknowledge that I was forgiven. She moved closer to a shelf in front of us and pulled a book out about halfway from its original position. She did not hand me the book, but rather pointed me to a book leaving the impetus on me to decide to follow her lead. I reached for the book and pulled it off of the shelf. She then moved to the right and started pulling more books halfway out to indicate which books she wanted me to read. I was overcome with a sense of "overload." The fact that she was pulling multiple books out caused me to realize I was not going to be able to remain focused for the time needed to understand all that she was telling me and remain in her presence.

I reached for the second book and as I held it, I decided to read the cover of the first book. The words were hazy and without form. I could see where words were supposed to be, but was having a hard time discerning the words. I have experienced this in the past and know that reading involves a greater amount of concentration and focus to discern words. I held the book to the light-source from above. I angled the book to try to catch a reflection from the printed title that could help me decipher the words (it was as if I needed to see the contrast in color and texture to discern the printed words from the surface of the book). Eventually the title came into

Rebirth I

view with the help of the light. At first I saw "Book of J……." and then it appeared to say "Book of Jonathan." But as I focused on the title, the word Jonathan transitioned into John.

There were several lines of smaller text beneath the title. I tried to discern the words but it was too strenuous of a task at that moment. There was one more large, bold word at the bottom of the cover that was the same size as the title. The word began with an "M." As I continued to hold it up into the light to try to discern the word, I thought the word was forming into the word "Matthew." But as soon as I began to form an interpretation of the word, the word "MICHAEL" came into view. I stopped and stared. The text at the top and the bottom of the cover were clear. "BOOK of JOHN"…."MICHAEL." I looked up at the angel beside me. She looked at me in intrigue. She knew I had read the words. My mind was racing. I said, "Am I? Are you?" With that question, a rush overcame me and everything faded away. I found myself in a room with a typewriter. I sat down and began writing about the experience. I was sure this was reality as I furiously documented the encounter. And then I awoke on Earth.

Upon waking, Bryan called. It was unusual to hear from him early in the morning. I groggily began to piece my words together. I shared with him the vision that had just occurred. He, too, had experienced a vision and needed to share it – a voice that came in the night. Everything I was saying was echoed back through a different lens of the voice's instructions.

The words that Bryan shared with me: "You're running down the hall, scribing books as you go. It is not enough to know. We must understand. It is not enough to understand. We must do!" Though it was a statement, the delivery and phrasing seemed to be posed as more of a rhetorical question – something that would be along the lines of "Are you going to treat life as a science experiment, or as a fiction novel where you are content to just sit back and read?" I am paraphrasing the question that Bryan shared with me, but that is the gist of the underlying message from the voice that came to him.

Of note, I received another call while I was on the phone with Bryan. The call was from Michael – a friend of mine that felt compelled to tell me that I should know about the story of Michael Roach, his book "The Diamond Cutter," and the school he created to help others learn the ways of the Tibetan monks. The brief overview I was given was that he was an ordained monk who practiced Buddhism for 25 years in a monastery during the first part of his journey. He now teaches in New York City. There are no such things as coincidences, and I know that having just experienced a vision with a book containing the name Michael on the cover, that having an unusual phone call from Michael pointing me to a book written by an author named Michael is a triune of angelic direction. This book will be the next book I will read.

November 9, 2013

I awoke from a vision that recurred multiple times in the night. There were four translucent spheres before me. Each

Rebirth I

sphere was connected to the next and dependent on the other. Each sphere represented one of the seven loci as well as a position in the seven character alignment of the Hebrew language. It is important to note that I thought the spheres represented locations of five steps on the scale. I cannot tell you if the first sphere was invisible and the other four spheres represented a one-to-one relationship, or if the fourth sphere represented spheres four and five. All I know is there was something greater than the representation of four spheres present.

The first sphere bounced into the second. The second bumped the third – which expanded and bounced into the fourth. Upon this sequence completing, I was given a word to recite. Throughout the night I remembered the word with clarity. It was one syllable – short and succinct. When the sun rose and I awoke from the vision, I went to write down the word and I lost the memory. Perhaps I will meditate upon it and have it come to me. But, for now it is lost. The word was not English – though it held a great significance. The illustration of the spheres was repeated in my vision so many times prior that I could not help but see it as a mantra. I repeated the sequence over and over again to memorize it – including the last word. But, again, for the time being, it is lost.

I had a second vision where I was standing in a perfect place – an abstract location, but perfect nonetheless. Before me was "the girl." She spoke in thoughts – not in words. She smiled. There was an overwhelming feeling of warmth and adoration from her to me (and I am sure from me to her). She told me, "I see you finally were able to get it parted." I looked at her quizzically. She said, "Your head – I see you were finally able to get it all of the way parted to one side." I smiled (thinking she was talking about my hair and struggles to grow it out at one point in my life) and said, "Yes. Yes I did. It took me several years, but yes. I was finally able to." She smiled. The vision ended.

Upon reflection of the experiences I realize I thought she was talking about my hair. Upon waking I knew she was talking about my mind – instantly. Visions are clouded moments of understanding through the experience, the situation, and in the way thoughts are transferred. However, once I had a chance to replay it back in my mind, I knew she was talking about my mind. She said "head" and nodded toward my forehead. She was talking about the distinct separation of mind, body and spirit, and the ability to discern the separation – something I have been struggling with. My visions have ramped up in recent weeks which is a byproduct of figuring out the separation a little better than I have in the past.

November 10, 2013
Early Morning

I had a vision of being in a house/hall. There were people everywhere. I was lost in the moment. By my side was "the girl" – with blonde hair. There were others around me. All of the people seemed very familiar, but I could not identify each person by name when I awoke. Conversations were had, ar-

Rebirth I

guments were made. But mostly, I was in awe of the moment – lost in the richness of the vision and "the girl" beside me.

November 10, 2013

Phone call with Bryan

Bryan shared with me a vision he had from last night. His vision began in a house. The house was divided into two levels. There were plenty of people milling around. A man in a suit – sinister, balding on top of his head, Pakistani (or something similar in race) was standing before him. He told Bryan that he was not going to let it happen tonight. Bryan was confused. A beautiful man that Bryan identified as an angel tossed a plumb line over at the man in the suit standing before Bryan, where it ignited in light.

Bryan understood the man in the suit to be Lucifer trying to stop Bryan from conversing with the angels. Bryan's mother, my sister, and several other people from Bryan's past were present. Bryan's mother and my sister both attempted to seduce him. Bryan was disgusted and tried to get away from them. He knew Lucifer was playing tricks on him – attempting to create as much "noise" as possible to prevent him from progressing to any other divine locations.

I entered the room with a blonde girl – simple in appearance. She took off her shoe and started drawing circles in the sand that comprised the floor. She warned Bryan that this was just the beginning. Another man in a suit entered into the

The Written

room. He told Bryan to follow him because they did not have much time. The man was slender with wiry hair and wearing a blue suit. Per Bryan's description, it would be appropriate to assume it was the same man in a suit who led me through a vision a few nights prior – the vision where he introduced me to a girl that fit the very description of the girl Bryan described. This girl was also the same girl from the vision that I had tonight. In fact, the vision I had aligns to another viewpoint of Bryan's vision – same location, same feelings, same people and the same context of the conversations.

The man in the blue suit came to Bryan and dropped a plumb line in front of him. He then shared a word with Bryan. It was short and succinct. He was told that the word had no Hebrew equivalent. It was something along the lines of Vat, Vav, Tav, etc. Bryan kept repeating the letters V and T to me in a one-syllable word. He also thought it contained the image of an S or a serpent. The word held within it a meaning of great strength.

When the man in the suit said the word (coupled with a few others), Bryan was put to sleep – as if tranquilized for just a brief moment. When he awoke, the chaos had faded. The sun was up and the house was empty. I was asleep in a corner, his mother was asleep in a corner, my sister was asleep in a corner. The girl that was with me was still standing in the same location – she had not moved. She told Bryan to be ready – more was about to happen.

Bryan was whisked away by a man. He told Bryan that they did not have long. Bryan looked around. He was standing

Rebirth I

in the middle of a garden. Before him was a tree that was cut in half and had a branch extended. The tree was smoldering. He reached out to touch the tree. The man told him not to touch it and said, "Don't you remember what happened the last time you touched it?" Bryan asked where they were. The man told Bryan to think hard – that he had been there before. Bryan asked, "Is this the Garden?" The man said, "Yes," and to "look now because they would not have long."

Bryan looked around and saw a blue body of water to his left with two distinct hues. The colors were intoxicating. The aromas were so rich, so pure. On top of the body of water were a series of great inventions. The first was a carpenter's square, and then there was a yin-yang carved into a rock. Following it, there was the great pyramid, a complex gear resembling the Antikythera Mechanism, and finally a translucent silicon circuit board complete with the chips. The man told Bryan he could know anything – but to be quick. Bryan looked to his right and saw a contraption that looked much like a tube extending upward. It was old, iron and with large rivets. There was a hatch-like door on the outside with a port to view inside. There was also a smaller tube extending at a 45° angle up and out from the tube itself. Bryan asked what it was. The man told Bryan, "Well, we are still working on that. No one has run with it yet. It is a time device. It is yours if you would like it." Bryan looked over at another object. It was around this time that the man told Bryan that his time was running out. Suddenly, there was a great light. Bryan awoke.

The Written

After talking with Bryan, we took notice that he and I shared these visions and the characters in the visions. He was also looking at the same time machine that I have witnessed in several visions. While I have not described the machine to Bryan beyond the vague terms of a "time machine," the device sounded exactly like the one from my vision. I have asked him to draw it and send it to me.

November 14, 2013

I walked to a great gate in the company of two others. "The girl" was on my right and a friend from my earthly life named Michael S. was on her right. We stood at an entrance that resembled an entrance to a gated neighborhood. The structure was thick – well-built with heavy stone that glistened a pristine white. The gates were wrought iron. There was an entrance gate and an exit gate. We stood in front of a keypad-like device that was located in the median of the entrance and exit lanes. I punched the numbers, but the gate would not open. "The girl" told me she would take care of it. She pushed a button and a voice rang out. As they carried on a brief conversation, I wandered over to a hill and stood upon it looking down on the gate and the road. As she finished her conversation I could tell we were buzzed in.

The gate opened and we all began to walk down an extremely wide road that had a large green hill on the right. To the left were dense trees. I could tell I was in a neighborhood

Rebirth I

and I was curious about what the houses looked like, but did not see any in the beginning. The road wound up a slight incline and wrapped behind the hill on my right. As we walked up the street, I began to hear music playing. It was simple but elegant, piano intertwined with strings. It reminded me of Christmas, but not any song I was familiar with. I shared with "the girl" and Michael how much I Loved the neighborhood – how the music was so pleasant. As we began to approach a house on the left I noticed that it began to mist. It was very distinct. I could feel the fine coat of water around me.

Over the crest of the hill a man's face appeared. It was the same gray-haired man who I witnessed in my other vision – the one who had sided with my father on my carelessness. He looked at me and then at "the girl." I could tell he was skeptical about whatever was about to take place. But as he crested the hill, he looked at me with recognition. He introduced himself and greeted me, but not by name. He talked with Michael briefly and then took his right hand and patted Michael's chest. He said some words that carried the impression of, "It is going to be good from here. Have no worries."

He then welcomed us into his home. It was large, but not as big as the other houses in the neighborhood. Another girl who I perceived to be his wife welcomed us into his living room where Michael, myself, and the man sat down. The table was long and I sat in the middle – Michael to my right, the man to my left. My intention was to make small talk and introduce Michael to this man. I felt that since I was welcomed into his house once before, that he could see the goodness in

The Written

Michael. As the man asked me questions, I talked about business, life, and lessons learned. It seemed as if we spoke for about an hour, and I knew our time was limited. Try as I may, I was unable to turn the conversation over to Michael. Eventually the man excused himself from the table for a few minutes. While he was gone, I told Michael to be patient, that I would make the introduction. But the man never returned. I became nervous that I was not going to be able to introduce Michael. And then the vision ended.

I found myself in the void where I sat down to write about the experience. I typed furiously recalling every detail. As I typed for what seemed like hours, I became aware that this area was not reality and then I awoke in my bed. This seems to be a recurring theme in my visions – where I exit them into a void to document them, to relive the moment over and over so I can recall it.

Upon the recognition that I had been in a vision, I immediately tried to force myself back into it. I pleaded to the angels to be patient with me – that I was finding my way back. I eventually found myself back in the house – though it took some time. When I arrived it was empty. I wandered around the house looking for the man. At one point some other guys entered the house. They too were looking for him. I thought they were his sons. They eventually made themselves comfortable in the living room, but I continued to search. I never found him and eventually the vision faded.

Rebirth I

November 14, 2013

Just talked with my earthly friend Michael. He told me how he had a bizarre dream last night. He said he was very aggressive and that it was a violent dream. He said that was unusual for him because he never experiences these types of things. But what is interesting is that last night I could not manage to turn the conversation over to Michael so he could chat with the man while we were sitting around the table. It seems that the place I took Michael was a place he had not been and struggled with the concept mentally. I could not turn the experience over to him because he struggled with his ascent into that level of vibration. Michael went on to explain that he never dreams and that this experience was extremely unusual for him. For me, this is the second time my spiritual interactions in the heavens transcended the earthly plane.

November 15, 2013

As I closed my eyes to go to sleep, I was immediately in another location. It was a busy environment – city-esque. A man in a suit bustled right by me. He turned and looked over his shoulder and said, "See? We are always here watching you. You also have the ability to be here anytime." The next part of his communication was done via impressions and not audible words. He told me [and anytime it is non audible, it is somewhat paraphrased], "You can leave your body anytime and be

The Written

in both places at once. Your brain will keep you yoked between the two worlds, but you have the ability to walk in both places simultaneously." I immediately awoke.

November 16, 2013

Today in the heavens I met Richard for lunch. I took him to a potential location for the Sonalkiss center. No one was in the office, so we wandered back to the room we were going to use. There was one wall that was basically a giant chalkboard. We began to write our thoughts and ideas onto this board. Some simple, some abstract – but the point was for us to write what we felt would be good in the moment. Suddenly a girl's voice called out, "Hey! What are you guys doing here? You know you should (points at her watch)…" I took it to mean "call first" but in retrospect she was signaling the shortness of remaining time for the interaction.

At that moment, a man walked in. I wandered out of the room to talk with both of them. I thanked them both again for the opportunity and explained we were just using the moment to write down ideas…that we were appreciative of having the space for Sonalkiss. He said it was okay, that we had just caught them off guard. He motioned for me to walk back into the room. When I walked back in, the wall that we were writing ideas upon was filled floor to ceiling with abstract and concrete concepts. The writing had a sense of completion to it. I immediately saw the all seeing eye on a pyramid, the symbols

Rebirth I

of the masons, and many other symbols of the occult. As I gazed upon the wall I tried to determine if Richard had written all of this or where it could have come from. One phrase on the board was written very large and took up the space of five or six other drawings. That phrase was written in a font style from the 1950s/60s/70s. It said, "waierliner aircraft <something>." I reread it several times and received the impression of "war craft" though the word said "aircraft."

Suddenly a formless man hustled in and set down a globe on a stand that was tilting with a rod coming through its poles. He made no eye contact. The object was about five feet tall and made of gold. Suspended from the rod was a plumb line. I recognized what it was and thought it was "ridiculously awesome." I walked back out of the room. The man that I had been speaking to before mentioned that he did not think I would have found the significance in the object that was just set down, but that clearly I had grasped the higher concept that it illustrated. The man started performing pseudo-yoga stretches. He placed one foot on my shoulder as he moved into a difficult posture. He then pulled that foot off of my shoulder and was basically levitating before me. Around that time the vision faded.

For a brief moment I returned. I walked outside. The sun was setting and a road was winding down and around a verdant green pasture on its right. Trees lined the road's left side. It was the same geometry of the landscape from my previous vision, but leading down a hill instead of up a hill. The sky was a fiery pink with bursts of yellow. Beautiful.

The Written

November 21, 2013

Last night I walked among angels and for a brief moment spoke with God. I awoke around 4:00 a.m. and was the most swirly-disoriented I have ever been. The experience was so beautiful and magnificent – I was there, and then I was right back on Earth. The disorientation caused me not to be able to recount any detail beyond the feeling I had which was "beautiful" and "a lot of light." But I can so clearly recall walking among angels – their tall silhouettes against a blinding background. The ground was an impossible cloud-like formation.

November 22, 2013

Today I called Bryan to share with him the vision from the previous night. When he answered the phone he could barely speak. As it turns out, he had just sent me a text as I was calling that said he had been diagnosed with "allergic rhinitis, acute pharyngitis, bilateral conjunctivitis, severe sinusitis, and pink eye." He could barely make a sound. When we began talking, I could not tell if he was crying or emotional, or just sick. I spoke most of the time, sharing my vision and eventually we circled around to a conversation I had with Daniel recently where we discussed how his first dream in forever occurred after a conversation we had. In that conversation I told him that when he asks God with an open mind and an open spirit, He will deliver. I told Bryan that I would have to be

Rebirth I

careful with the situation because I do not want Daniel seeing me as the reason why he had his first vision. Though the moment was extremely spiritual, I know that God opened Daniel's eyes – not me.

I went on to explain to Bryan that I finally understood how God works through a person. I used to think that divine miracles were something that would have to be done physically – something a person has an awareness of how to control. It is a concept I have been wrestling with a lot recently. But I told Bryan that now I understood that I have zero control – no awareness of how it would be done, but God would come when there is faith. This is a concept that breaks the analytical part of my mind, but one that I would have to be comfortable with.

As Bryan and I talked, he struggled to get out any words. He told me how much it hurt. I told him that he might as well talk because speaking was not going to make it any worse – it may hurt, but it would not make it worse. It was important that we continued the spiritual conversation. We spoke for about ninety minutes total, and throughout the conversation Bryan's voice began to clear up. By the end of the conversation, Bryan's voice sounded perfect. He had no congestion, no pain. I made sure that Bryan knew this was the work of God healing him. He agreed whole-heartedly. He works in a hospital and understands the scope of viruses and the severity of his diagnosis. It was clear that someone who had just been diagnosed with all of those ailments just an hour or so before would not be able to heal that quickly under any natural circumstance. We shared in the joy of being witness to such a moment. This was the second miracle of God's work.

November 23, 2013

Bryan called me this morning to confirm his health. He sounded perfect. He also said that his pink eye was completely gone – nothing lingering or appearing in the night as most sicknesses will do. This was confirmation of the second miracle of God's work.

November 23, 2013

Today after yoga, I was heading home and decided to stop and pick up lunch. Because I had about thirty minutes until the restaurant opened, I decided to stop at Wal-Mart first to pass some time. When I went to the front door, I was stopped by a boy passing out half-sheets of paper with a list of items he was hoping people would purchase for his Eagle Scout project. I told him I would consider it and went inside. After I walked in, I turned left to head to the section that had protein bars (I was running low).

As I was walking toward the protein bar section I heard a woman behind me say, "Excuse me sir. Do you work here?" I stopped in my tracks because I was the only person in the vicinity of the voice. I turned behind me to see an elderly lady pushing a shopping cart in my direction. I asked her if she was

Rebirth I

talking to me – she indicated that she was. I told her, "I'm sorry. No ma'am. I do not." I turned to continue walking but stopped again. Something was off. Having just come from yoga, I was wearing a pair of sneakers, black kung-fu pants, a black and gray pullover and a bandana tied around my head to keep my hair and the sweat out of my eyes. My hair was still wet and disheveled from the sweaty workout I had just left. I also had on headphones. When I walked by the boy passing out the papers, I had paused the music and had not turned it back on. Though, to a bystander I appeared to be listing to music and oblivious to the world around me. So in this moment, I realized that the question I was asked by the lady could not have been asked to a more out-of-place person. I clearly was not an employee, nor should I have even heard her question had my music been turned on. And instantly I realized it was not her voice calling out. It was God's.

I turned back and said, "I know I don't work here, but is there anything I can help you with?" She smiled. She had the bluest eyes I have ever seen. Her eyes spoke words of spiritual recognition. She said that I could. She was looking for the cards and Christmas section. I pointed her straight ahead and said, "You are going in the right direction. Just keep going straight ahead and you will see the cards on your left and Christmas section straight in front of you. I may not work here, but I've been here enough to help you out." She smiled and thanked me and went on.

I wandered through the store to the back where I sorted through the list to determine what item I should get to help the

The Written

boy who had greeted me. As I walked through each of the sections that contained the items, I noticed that everyone around me was carrying the same piece of paper and trying to find the items to help the boy. It was one of the warmest moments I have witnessed. I would not have imagined that so many people would be willing to help out. I decided that the boy was more than taken care of by God, so I continued passing time in the store.

I eventually headed up to the register to pay for the handful of items I had picked up. In front of me, there was a mother and daughter buying a full shopping cart's worth of Thanksgiving items. It was easy to tell they were not well off. As they were checking out, they made sure to purchase a large amount of cigarettes. In this moment, I wrongfully thought to myself, "How could they spend so much on something that was so unhealthy for them?" As they went to check out, the total came to $102.10. The daughter asked the mother, "Do you know that the total is $100?" The mother became flustered and handed her a debit card. She asked if she could charge $80 on it. The cashier acknowledged, but the card declined.

The mother and daughter became frustrated – the mother nearly throwing a fit in the store. The mother asked if they could try running it for $75 and if it didn't go through, she would leave. The cashier tried and the card declined again. The daughter was visibly upset with the mother. The mother was throwing a fit in the store at this point indicating that there was a problem with the card. I strongly thought about

Rebirth I

just paying for their groceries – and perhaps that is what I should have done. But, I kept hearing the part of the conversation about cigarettes in my head and somehow the gesture did not feel right. I am usually generous in situations like this (almost every time) – but this time it was different. I could not put my finger on it, but I knew I was not supposed to help them.

After they left, the woman behind me began talking to me about the situation with the mother and daughter. Again, I had on my headphones so I knew something was causing her to speak to me. I explained to her what I had witnessed. The woman showed so much compassion for the situation. She told me how the mother was just embarrassed. She explained how hard these times are financially for others and that she probably didn't even know how much she was buying and then was embarrassed she did not have enough money for it. She then said, "There is nothing to be embarrassed about. It happens to people, and others should understand that. I feel bad for them." I nodded my head in recognition to what she was saying.

As I left, I realized that everything about that encounter was the equivalent of what I would experience in a vision to catch my attention. In the beginning of a vision, there is a queue – something that stands out as "off" and not like reality. This helps bring a person into awareness of the vision. This happened to me with the blue-eyed lady. She was a messenger queuing me in on something I needed to witness. All of the events following that encounter were there for me to be an observer – to see the mechanics to life and understand how others see and experience the world. All the people I witnessed helping the boy with his project, the embarrassed mother and daughter, and finally the lady behind me that helped share with me the lesson of that moment. While most people may see this as just random events in a Wal-Mart, nothing is random. And for those who have experienced the other side, seeing the same happen in the human experience is a moment that will forever be etched in my mind. The heavens and the Earth are one and the same – just depending on which set of eyes you are viewing it from. Will you see the earthly walk as a divine experience, or will you see it as a mundane yin to Heaven's yang? For me, this was the most visual queue I have had.

November 25, 2013

I awoke this morning from a vision that is still a little hazy, though I managed to hang on to the important details. While I experienced the vision, it was as vivid as could be imagined. It began with me having an understanding of the future. Much earlier in my journey, I would have equated this to a "bouncing in and out of a dream within a dream." But, now that I have been able to more finely tune my understanding of the experience, I realized that I knew the ending of the vision before it began – but, this time, there was a lesson to be learned in the experience of the linear aspect of the vision.

Rebirth I

My vision began with the awareness of an impending ending – a change in direction. I also was aware of the setting being in the future. I found myself in a heavenly country landscape where I was escorted around by both a male and a female angel. The female angel (the recurring "the girl" I reference) was the most interactive with me. In the beginning she showed me several cameras/devices and asked me my thoughts on them. I began rattling off technical details as she handed me one particular camera that she said that she used.

I looked at it and told her instinctively that it was a very good camera and better than what I had to work with. The camera had a resolution written on the bottom of the device of 3120 x 720 (which I knew was not a great resolution and an odd perspective ratio). I usually struggle to read in such vivid projections due to the high amount of swirly/disorienting energy associated with the moment, so I think the numbers were intended by the angels to test how rooted in the vision I was – to see if what I was to experience would stick and come back with me when I returned to Earth. At the time of the interaction with the camera, I had not fully differentiated the vision from earthly reality. Regardless, I apparently was rooted enough to continue on.

In the next part of the vision I was given three signs of the end of whatever I was about to experience. The first was the image of a lion's face. The second was an image of a barn. The third was an image of me in some type of a uniform and handcuffs (I originally thought it was a prison uniform). The next part of the vision continued with me going to a home in

The Written

the wooded countryside. The house already had people in it, though I understood the house to be mine. I saw several people that I recognized – my grandmother, my grandfather, a young man in his early twenties (though I do not know his name).

As I walked around the house, I interacted with everyone, but I had a sad feeling of the impending ending. People continued to gather at the house. Eventually, the gathering became more of a social party that seemed to be more "out of control" than I would have liked. Fearing the ending from the signs I had been given, I thought that something would happen where I would be taken from my family for something that occurred at this social gathering. The angels stayed with me the whole time.

In a banquet hall, the atmosphere was calmer than the rest of the house. This is where my grandparents were mingling with others. I was immediately overcome with sadness when I entered the room. I walked over to my grandmother and gave her a huge embrace and told her how much I Loved her. She was surprised, but hugged me back and comforted me. I walked to my granddad and did the same. He hugged me back and comforted me as well. I felt like not only was I about to have to change directions in my life, but that my grandfather was going to be experiencing the same thing soon. I walked back to the angels where I embraced the female and she just held me to bring me peace. I explained to her that I knew the ending was coming.

Rebirth I

That part of the vision faded into the next where it was the following morning. Most of the people were asleep, but I heard someone enter the house. I looked through the peephole of the door to the room I was in and saw a light shining down the hallway toward the door. I saw a group of two or three police officers. As they got to the door, I opened it and let them in. The female officer started explaining that they had "noticed that I had left a crack in the door and that is why they were there." I became frustrated with them and told them not to lie to me. I told them I already knew why they were there and that I opened the door for them – they could not have "noticed a crack in the door." I told them it was impossible because I saw them and opened the door. I told them that it was fine they were there – just to tell me the truth. That is all I ever want. The officers proceeded to ask me several questions and left.

I turned to the female angel (who was still with me) and asked why they left. I told her I did not understand because I knew I was going to get arrested/taken away. She never answered. I walked around the house and told everyone we had to leave. The angel and I walked into a room to get the young man I had identified earlier. He was in bed with a beautiful brunette girl. When I entered the room, I was overcome with the emotion of Love that the couple shared. I could not help but smile. The angel smiled too. I told the young man we had to go. The boy looked at the girl and they started saying the saddest goodbyes. She looked at me with eyes of sadness, Love, and longing. My heart melted for her. I could tell they

Loved each other deeply. The girl hopped on top of him and started kissing him passionately. I turned with the angel and walked out of the room giving them time to properly say goodbye. All I could do was smile because of how memorable the moment would be for each of them.

    I told the angel that it was important to give him a moment because I could tell how happy they were and how hard it was for them to say goodbye. Eventually our group was formed and we left the house. We walked up a winding road and found ourselves on top of a hill. I looked around to survey the area. In front of me was a barn in a pasture with a beautiful sunset behind it. I knew my final moments were drawing to a close.

    I looked to my right and I saw the house we had just left had a giant face of a lion on the outside of it. Coming down the road in our direction were the officers that showed up at the house earlier. When they reached us, I stepped away from the angel and asked them if it was time. They said it was. As I stood there, my clothes transformed into a prisoner's uniform and my hands were handcuffed in the front. The angel walked over to me to see if I was okay. I told her that while I did not understand why it had to be this way, I knew this was God's plan for me. In those moments I felt stripped of all earthly possessions and knew that it was just me and the garment I was wearing. Everything that would happen from that point forward was strictly between me and God with no earthly possessions getting in the way. I thought that it must be God's will for me to serve as a witness to other "prisoners" where I

Rebirth I

was not to be distracted by any possessions. But — I felt strong. I felt I was a vessel for God's will, strengthened by Him. While I struggled to understand why I was being "arrested," I knew there was a purpose and without question, I found myself looking forward to the opportunity that I was given. As the angel stood in front of me, the lion's face on the outside of the house behind her was bold and large — filling my entire periphery. It was a moment that I could paint a million pictures of the imagery and never do it justice. This was our heavenly goodbye. I turned to be escorted away and everything faded away.

November 26, 2013

Messages I wrote to Bryan today regarding another vision I had just experienced:

"After digging into the two numbers I was given as 'camera resolution,' I have arrived at the following: the third number to complete the series is either 6420 or 9750. I am unsure what it means yet, but it is an 8th dimensional triangle assuming our spirit functions on the 7th level — or possibly the three points to create the beginning of a spiral to traverse the spheres.

When working through the concept of the camera resolution, the width/height = 4.33333333. At first I thought that was nothing significant. After figuring out the triads that I texted you courtesy of Pythagoras, I did a quick search for the significance of 4.333333 in science. I arrived at one interesting math equation: (4x5+6)/(double)(2x3). This was from a CSC121 class for Java. Maybe no significance, maybe some. You can

The Written

remove the idea of (double) because that just means that you want the denominator to produce a decimal instead of a whole number. So the math is (4x5+6)/(2x3). Anyway, maybe nothing....I agree. But let's continue on. So I clicked the next link that showed up in Google and got to the page I linked to below. Read the numbers, the concept, and everything about the problem. Set 54 = 5+4 which = 9. Problem number 7. SEVEN. Now see that the number 4.33333 is used to indicate a diameter. Kind of a bizarre number to pick, huh? Also, the water is flowing at 8m/s. I just texted you these numbers indicated 8th dimension, right? And we are talking about water....the significance there should be apparent. The beginning radius is .13 meters. Again – another Divine key. So to review: problem title: 5+4 = NINE. Problem SEVEN. Speed of water EIGHT m/s. Diameter of pipe = 4.33333333. Radius at the beginning of flow = THIRTEEN meters. Buried in this equation is part of the reason why I was given those particular numbers.... MORE INTERESTING: I just backed out of the test to see what the subject matter was: 'Introductory Problem Sets, Fluids and Thermodynamics and Waves'"

November 26, 2013

I asked God if I'm supposed to build a time machine because that sure is what everything seems to be pointing to and I just needed to make sure I'm not being crazy. God himself replied, "Noah. I asked Noah to build an ark. I am asking you now." I asked, "Where am I to begin because I'll need some direction. I'm not quite sure where to start." God replied, "Noah didn't know where to start either. I have given you all that you need." Then, there was an implied directive to study

Rebirth I

those lessons I was led to today. And just that quickly, I was alone. I then realized this was my first full conversation with God. Thoughts of Abraham filled my head – how he heard the voice of God and how he conversed with him...not in visions, but in conversation. Then I understood.

November 29, 2013

I found myself standing in a large building. I had the impression I was in a hospital, though the surroundings would not fit that description. The lighting was blue/green and everyone was wearing white. While I was wandering around the halls, "the girl" came up to me. I didn't recognize her due to the settings, but it was clearly her. She tried to get my attention though I continued to act shyly around her. Eventually the brunette girl came up and began talking to her. They were both trying to get my attention by being flirty in front of me. They would casually talk and then turn to me to ask my opinion.

When it was clear I was not paying them any attention, they began acting more comically in front of me to help me realize where I was. The brunette girl began talking about her chin hair. The blonde girl touched her chin – they giggled back and forth and asked me what I thought about it. They found it humorous, but I still wasn't queued into the moment. Eventually a man came up to me and dropped something near my leg. Suddenly I writhed in pain. I looked down and on my leg was a giant cat-sized ant biting my leg. The ant was black and on its tail was a large red hourglass. At the time, all I could think about was the horror of being bitten by that large of a black widow spider. I didn't clue in to the message of my time being limited (the hourglass) and to snap into it.

    I tried to shake the ant off of my leg, but it had burrowed itself in. Eventually, I was able to pull it off of me, but the girls had left my presence. I wandered around the hospital asking for help – but everyone looked at me as if I had lost my mind. At one point I wandered up a set of stairs and into a lounge. I had walked through this room previously with a large group of people. This is where the girls first appeared. This time though, there were just a couple of people in the room. They appeared to be janitors – or people cleaning up the area after everyone had left. I asked them where everyone went. They told me that everyone had to go. They offered no explanation, but I understood it to mean that I "missed my window" to interact with the angels.

December 5, 2013

    I saw "the girl" walking toward me though, for some unknown reason, I tucked my head to hide my excitement to see her. This sequence repeated itself many times, but in different locations as I wandered through the Heavens. Eventually she passed by one last time, came up directly to me and said, "Why do you keep doing that?!" I asked, "What? You mean

Rebirth I

tuck my head? I didn't realize I was doing that." She looked at me, frustration in her face. She didn't say another word, but I knew that I was frustrating her by not acknowledging her. From my viewpoint, I definitely wasn't ignoring her. On the contrary, I was extremely excited to see her, but when she came near I had to compensate for the great feeling of Love that she radiated. For the first time that I can recall (though this feeling seems to have manifested over the last couple of days in my visions), I felt timid around her. I felt an uneasiness of not being able to communicate because of the strength she radiated toward me and the feelings I felt toward her. It would be tantamount to the first time a boy likes a girl in the human experience. Words fall short, and emotions are uncontrollable. I don't know if this means that my growth in spirit is crossing into a stage equivalent to puberty in the human experience, or if there is another set of unknown circumstances causing the questions. But whatever the case may be, it was extremely vivid, though uneventful in activity beyond "the girl" appearing time and time again.

December 9, 2013

The vision I had today was one that built on one I could not fully recall from last week – so the vision in and of itself must be significant. I was on an island (part of a chain of islands). Each island was slender and long, but small enough that they could be traversed end-to-end in a short amount of

The Written

time. This chain of islands led away from a larger island containing a large, dormant volcano. Just from the setting, I equated the scenario to be Hawaii, but no location names were mentioned. The waters were crystal clear with a hint of azure blue. The sands were as white as they could be. The grass was a vivid green.

I was standing on the island with Bryan and "the girl." She asked me, "How many moons are there?" I instinctively said, "One." She said, "No. You are not where you think you are. Look again." I looked into the sky. The sun was setting over my right shoulder, so I must have been facing south. The horizon was a dim pink. The setting sun reflected with a pink and gray hue off of the bottom of the few clouds in the west. As I looked into the night sky, I observed two very small, but visible moons. They were crescent shaped – resting in a bowl-like angle. As soon as I saw the two smaller moons, I exclaimed, "Four. There are four moons." She said, "Yes. Yes there are four moons." I began to point out the two I saw. Bryan told me not to miss the closest moon that was half way behind a cloud. I looked at it and said, "This must be the real moon."

I looked above it and there was a slightly smaller version located to the north of the moon. I said, "No, this must be it. Hmmm. No. I think I had it right the first time." "The girl" giggled. I placed my pinky finger into the sky as if to mimic the fingernail appearance of the smaller moons. I looked at Bryan and said, "Isn't it cool? Look. All four moons and they all have the same shape." As I looked over at Bryan, I could see some-

Rebirth I

thing else had his attention. I looked over to the left to see a giant sphere hurdling through the sky in the direction of the volcanic island in the west. The sphere was spinning in a clockwise motion and looked like a cast metal version of Earth. Bryan exclaimed, "Oh no!" We looked at each other and I said, "This is it. We need to get to higher ground."

It was in those moments I could envision the giant sphere crashing into the volcano causing a tidal wave that would wipe out all life on the islands. But I could also see the collision triggering the volcano to erupt in a way larger than has ever been witnessed by mankind. This eruption would wipe out all humanity. I immediately recalled the helicopters that I had purchased and stored on another island. These helicopters were small, two-seaters that I purchased in my last vision (the one that I could not recall). In short, all I could recount from that vision was that I was on this same island and had purchased a helicopter for some unknown reason. Bryan, "the girl," and I ran East toward the next island over. When we got there, "the girl" helped us pull the helicopters out from storage. One helicopter was red. One was blue. I was really curious as to why the helicopters looked slightly different (as if they were different models).

I flashed into a vision of a conversation with the guy from whom I purchased the helicopters. I asked him why they were different. He said, "We had one model on hand and thought it was more important for you to have the helicopter than to wait on us ordering two matching versions. The one we ordered was not in stock, so we ordered a nicer model for you at no additional cost. Again, we thought it was more important for you to have the pair, than wait on the set to match."

I flashed out of the vision and back to the setting on the island. I knew that Bryan and I had to fly up into the sky. But, I was unsure how we would survive the ash plume from the volcano. However, I knew that the impending tidal wave would drown us, so we must go North. I looked at Bryan and told him we need to fly to the big island (the one with the volcano) to save anyone that is there. I said we should also make sure to take enough clothes with us to survive. I told Bryan to fly right. He hopped in the blue helicopter and flew off. I hopped in the red helicopter and flew to the left. I knew I would have to fly high into the event horizon of the plume, but I wasn't sure if I was supposed to fly above it, of just into it. At this time I awoke.

December 10, 2013

Bryan shared with me his vision of encountering a spirit he had never encountered before. His impression was that the spirit carried negative energy with it. It identified itself as John of Abraxas and told Bryan that it would always find Bryan – that there was no escaping his involvement in his life.

Rebirth I

December 11, 2013

Today I met with Daniel. He shared with me the dream that he had the night after we last met. It was the first dream that Daniel had ever experienced in his recent memory – and was something he asked God to receive. Between our last meeting and this meeting, Daniel and I spoke once on the phone where he shared with me that he had experienced his first vision, but it did not make a lot of sense. I told him to continue to ask and he would be granted more.

Today he shared with me that he had three additional visions since that conversation. As he explained them, I was able to interpret them with clarity for him. To Daniel, they were seemingly random dreams. To me, they were the first experiences of understanding his rebirth. In one he was in a room with a group of other people. There were guards blocking the exits. As he wandered around with his wife, they eventually found a way out. As they began their exit from the location, another guard stopped him from going anywhere. The dream changed to him sitting in a house with a woman making sure he did not go anywhere. This was "the girl." I did not tell him anything about her because it is up to him to continue to understand who she is. I did not even acknowledge that I was aware of who she was. I just listened.

In another vision Daniel experienced walking through a nice neighborhood with a road that wound up and to the right. I am sure it was the same location I have described in detail many times past, but again I did not acknowledge I had also experienced these moments. I listened to his story about encountering a group playing basketball in a poor section at the beginning of the neighborhood and how he met other individuals while he was there. Daniel was allowed into the gates, but he is still not aware. I have been unsure of what all to tell him because it is all new to him (and he has to understand on his own without being told). But, I did share with Daniel that these visions were extremely important in understanding where he is in respect to his spiritual journey. God – I ask for you to speak through me in ways that Daniel needs to hear, for he is a child of Yours and is trying to find his way home.

December 13, 2013

This morning I heard a voice from the heavens. It spoke only one word: PRVL. I heard it with "ah" sounds for vowels to indicate something along the lines of PROVOL or PRAVAL. As the voice spoke, it was indicated that this was a location – the name for the Heaven that I have been allowed to visit. As the words resonated within, an image of the Earth held together in the 8-sphere cube appeared. The central sphere (9th sphere) was glowing in a hue of azure blue-green that is unable to be reproduced on Earth.

My understanding was that this was the location (or possibly just a location of) PRVL. I saw it as the Earth and Moon were in direct alignment with the sun and I became aware that manifestation of **PRVL** occurs in the same lensing principles of the 8-sphere. When the sun and moon hold the Earth in equidistance, the lensing of **PRVL** is most easily available to the spirit. This is also why as the sun rises on Earth, the sun is often setting in **PRVL**. It is to indicate the relative location of Earth's side in respect to the sun and **PRVL**'s side with respect to the moon. It is also important to understand that **PRVL** in Hebrew (though not a word that is found in any ancient texts) would loosely mean "the breath/wisdom of the spiritual mountain that nails/drives the spirit in a way unto how a shepherd tends a flock of sheep through guidance."

After reflecting on the vision and researching the word, I've learned the word **PRABAL** in Hindi is used to describe god figures – much like Aleph-Tav in Hebrew. It does not have a literal translation but could best be used to illustrate "strength." Typically it is used to describe Hanuman. The story of Hanuman talks about him taking the top of a mountain in the Himalayas for the Lord because he could not determine what the proper herb was to bring back from the mountain.

December 13, 2013

11:25 a.m.

In my first experience of the morning, I was in a city park with a black guy and several other bystanders. The park was paved with benches and fountains all around. He kept demonstrating how four circles ratcheting 45° to the left created four more behind it. Those four are hidden but were extra important. They were not equidistant. They appeared to be spaced far enough apart where the circles appeared as eight dots around the edge of a square. When the guy sat down, the four circles overlaying his hind side and legs revealed four more spheres rotated at 45°. People kept remarking "I bet he won't lose those. They are his favorite." One circle that appeared showed up on his rear right pocket when viewed from behind. It was orange. At the end, he kept asking me if I wanted "two for one." I said what are you taking about? He said, "Two flat pizzas for $1." He emphasized the crust popped up three inches instantly when heated. He explained that the pizzas just needed to be put on a tray which was described to me as a square mesh tray to place the pizzas directly upon when placed into the oven.

In an additional experience, there was something important about the word **PHLN** (pronounced philahn). Another subsequent experience involved a letter given to me by a follower. There was a very long tube. I was told that he would follow me because he was tired of the math not working out and he knew that while the math wouldn't work out, the solution would. He offered for me to come across the street (presumably to his office) but continued to emphasize that he was tired of the math. This was on the heals of **PHLN** which could mean phi lan where phi is why math won't work out and LAN indicates something else.

Rebirth I

After researching the word PHLN, I now believe it stood for Philon, an ancient Greek architect written about by Vitruvius. I believe PHLN introduced himself to me and that the setting I experienced was ancient Greece (all paved with white cement/stone and the white fountains). After doing some additional research, I have now begun to read The Ten Books of Architecture by Vitruvius as I believe my encounter with PHLN was a pointer to this book.

December 16, 2013

Though the details are foggy, Bryan handed me a Blu-ray box. The movie inside wasn't the same as the slip cover (which I pulled off and proceeded to joke about with him). The Blu-ray contained ten discs in vertical sleeves. The discs were translucent. I flipped over the cover and it said "007." I assumed it was the James Bond package, but it only contained 10 movies all dating to when I was a child or younger. The movie names were not familiar. There were both numbers and names on each of the discs. I am sure that the intention of the vision was to remember the numbers and names so I could research the message being told to me. Unfortunately I have been unable to recall the names or numbers in enough detail to make sense of it. I also did not write it down immediately upon waking – which is why the details are foggy.

December 17, 2013

Quite possibly, this is one of the grandest moments that has occurred to me during the course of my journey. As I struggled to fall asleep last night, I made sure to have a few extra conversations with God. I assumed my struggle to fall asleep was the restlessness of my conscience from the previous Saturday. I have prayed for forgiveness for my lack of spiritual stature, but this time was different for some reason. I've continued to have a weight placed upon my chest from decisions I made. From the outside, most would not have noticed the stumble I made on my journey. But Saturday I allowed myself to stray from the path that I have been on. Though, like I said – on the outside, it would not have appeared that I had strayed. For me though, any slight waver from the straight and narrow path that is before me becomes greater in severity to my soul. For as a child, more grace is given to stumble. But as a child grows into an adult, the grace to stumble becomes more severely restricted. It has become so that at times I struggle to discern where that line is when just experiencing life on Earth. But anyway – I digress.

This struggle is my own battle and not one that deserves more writing than I already have. So – as I have continued to experience this weight over the last couple of days, and the restlessness of my sleep last night, I asked God to help with some sign to help bring me back to the spiritual grounding I had experienced prior to this past Saturday. As this journal

Rebirth I

will indicate, I rarely ask for anything – but when I do, there is a purpose in guidance and hope. This time was no different, except that I was looking for acknowledgement of His forgiveness. It is not that I think God doesn't forgive sometimes, but rather that forgiveness must be earned from demonstrable acts of humbling oneself before God. And in my personal situation, I wasn't sure how to demonstrate spiritual stature and therefore unsure of how I could walk the walk of asking for forgiveness. So, I asked for a sign – something to help me get back mentally to where I need to be – so that I can demonstrate the walk to Him. Again, I want to emphasize that where I am on my journey comes with increasingly complex layers of spiritual direction and I have to learn – just as any other – how to continually sharpen and refine my spirit upon my walk. If I am not continuing to sharpen my spirit, the journey becomes stagnant, and that is the best way I can illustrate my struggle today. Stagnation leads to regression on the journey.

My prayer to God was the last thing I remember before I was able to fall asleep. During the night I never completely fell asleep, but I did drift in and out from time-to-time. Around 4:00 a.m. I had drifted off and heard a booming voice call out my name. I was so startled that my eyes popped open, wide-awake. I turned over to face the direction in my apartment where the voice originated. In my startled – albeit calm – state, I found myself staring at an angel. This angel was not glowing or a transparent manifestation. This angel was as human in form as anyone could be. The angel was hovering approximately 4 to 5 feet off of the ground flapping its wings with zeal.

The Written

The wings were so plush. I saw the moonlight streaming in from the window creating the shadows underneath the plush feathers as they moved in the air.

The angel did not make a sound. It was human in form, wearing a white robe. I would guess that it's height was somewhere between 5 ½ and 6 feet tall. The angels hair was dark brown. The angel faced East Northeast at 60° (as I measured with a compass this morning). From my perspective, I could only see a side view of the face. The angel had an austere expression and never looked my way. It was there to be seen by me, but not have interaction. I could not believe my eyes. The angel's form was so perfectly human – so perfectly real and tangible. All attempts at rationalizing how a spirit would appear before me were no longer applicable. I stared at the great angel before me, studying its wings and form. Slowly, it started to fade away; first the feet, then the body, then finally the wings and the face faded into nothing and everything at once. I rolled over in bed amazed at what I had just seen. As I began to fall asleep again, I heard my name called once again. I turned to look in the same place. This time I saw another faint, fading manifestation of the same angel – though it only lasted but a split second. This second calling was a spiritual message to help me know it was real. Today, I am humbled to have experienced a sign from God so great that I can't help but understand my place at the mercy of His great will and strength.

Rebirth I

December 18, 2013

Today during my meditation, I stood in the midst of a group of people from ancient Greece. While I could not see the features of anyone, I could clearly make out the voices. I was being read the words from something being notated. Hermes's name was mentioned, though I could not determine if Hermes was speaking, or Hermes was who was being addressed due to the statement saying "I, Hermes…" I cannot recall the rest of the words except for an utterance of the name Thoth. It was as if they were spoken in another language, but my mind interpreted them in English. I know very little about Hermes beyond the name, so I will continue to research this vision. This is the second time (including meeting PHLN) that I can say with confidence I experienced some sort of Greek-experience.

December 22, 2013

Bryan had a vision of being in Heaven for at least seven or eight months. He spoke with the black angel who took him up into the sky and told Bryan to jump. Bryan glided down and landed. People spoke about him. Bryan was referred to as "the one that the black man had taught to fly." All I could think of upon this description was his name, "Talon." The black man appeared to Bryan as a butler of a great mansion. He continued to speak to Bryan about a problem they have experienced.

The Written

They were able to build great things (such as airplanes made out of that same riveted metal that continues to recur in his visions after the time machine vision), but they did not understand the science. The man told Bryan that there was a problem with the intersecting timelines. Bryan shared with him the science of Physics and Chemistry, though the details of the conversation were vague to Bryan. He also mentioned two giggling girls were present in the heavens with him. When Bryan described this to me, I recalled my visions where the two girls giggled in front of me as they tried to get my attention. Eventually I recognized that if I told them I knew who they were, they would change form into their great angelic forms. As Bryan and I discussed the similarities, he brought up a video from Enya – "Caribbean Blue." Within the song, it mentions several Latin words that translate into each of the four winds, as well as one of the "lesser four" winds from the Southwest.

First Revelation

In the moments following this morning's experiences, I knew this was the mark of the end of Rebirth I. When I began journaling, this book did not have a name, nor had the book been defined as a book, much less part of a series of nine books. But as all of the writing started to fall into view, the names became evident; my understanding of God's intentions became much clearer. Without words, this particular experience was the moment that shifted my understanding of heavenly experiences and experiencing The One True Heaven. There truly are no words to describe the gravity of this moment, thus I have named it "First Revelation."

...

December 23, 2013

1:55 a.m.

I awoke from one of the most awe-inspiring experiences I have been allowed to have in the Kingdom. Though I experienced a much greater amount of time than I was allowed to bring back in words with me, what I can share is truly remarkable. I found myself standing among a group of about eight or

Rebirth I

nine others – all appearing relatively the same in age (somewhere in the mid-twenties to early-thirties). While everyone appeared the same age, I felt like a child among children. We listened to one elder speak. The location was one that I have been experiencing in greater frequency recently. The setting was in a park (or something similar) that appeared to be made of all alabaster. At first, I assumed I was standing in ancient Greece, but the more I observed and learned from the experience, I now can say with confidence that my experiences in Greece are most definitely inside the walls of Heaven. Now, though, I can justify that I have been to *The Heaven* described since the ancient of days, I had been hesitant to interpret any location up until now as anything other than "the heavens." There is a distinct reason in that the settings have been very fluid and undefined in physical stature, however much they have continued to recur in similar form within my visions. However, this newest setting holds within it something that cannot be put into words – a tangible location that is steeped in antiquity.

The awareness of its age and place in time are part of the reason I can define it as Heaven. But, more importantly, the sum of the experiences – especially one very specific experience that occurred during this moment – help define this location as something more than just "one of the heavens." As I stood amongst the group, I became extremely aware of my simultaneous spiritual and earthly divide. My mind raced with two specific questions. I tugged on the sleeve of the robe of the elder. He was taller than each of us, though not out-of-place in

First Revelation

height. The difference reminded me of being a small child next to an adult, but the visual appearance of the situation was manifested as everyone being relatively similar in height and age.

The elder had curly brown hair – about shoulder length. Around the crown of his head, he wore a slender crown that kept his hair out of his eyes. His skin was olive in complexion and he had dark brown eyes. His nose was flat and slightly hooked; very distinct in facial structure. He was slender, but not lanky in build. He wore a robe of white. As I tugged on his sleeve and gained his attention, he looked down upon me and smiled. I asked him if I could ask a question. He smiled and said, "Of course you can. What would you like to know?" I said, "Can you tell me where we are? I know I am not on Earth and I'm somewhere else. But, can you tell me – even just a general location?"

My voice echoed the words in a higher pitch – like that of a child's. He smiled and said, "Why yes I can. Do you not know where you are?" I was stunned. This is the first question, I was about to receive a direct answer to – and I foresaw it coming. I told him that I knew I was not on Earth, and I think I know, but I wanted to hear it from him. That was important to me." He looked at me as lovingly as anyone ever could and smiled. He said, "You are in His Kingdom." I looked in amazement. I asked, "Is this heaven?" He kept smiling and said, "Yes. Yes it is."

I was overcome with excitement. I asked his name – and while he told me, I was so overcome with excitement that his

Rebirth I

name left me in that moment. He was also the first person that had directly given me a name during any vision. I have been given names in the past, but not the name of the person with whom I was speaking. I have only been told the names of those I have interacted with in previous visions. This time was different. I asked the man if I could ask him one more question. He just kept smiling and laughing in amusement at me as he said, "Of course you can."

I asked him, "What am I? I mean, not who am I. I don't need to know my name. I don't need you to tell me that right now. I just really need to know – what am I? Can you tell me that?" He just kept smiling and said, "I weep be." I was very confused for the words did not sound like a word I knew. I asked him, "What is that?" He said, "Oh. You don't know?" I said, "No. Is everyone?" He replied, "They are one of two – but I can't recall the name of the other." He then stumbled through saying what the other word might be and sort of gave up on the word indicating it wasn't important and re-emphasized "I weep be." I repeated back to him, "I weep?" as I pointed to my eyes to symbolize crying. He smiled and said, "Yes. I weep."

I asked, "Am I weeping?" He smiled and then filled my head of an image of tears of happiness streaming down either side of a nose. I couldn't tell if it was my nose, or his, because the emphasis was on the tears. As that image faded, I felt resolve in his answer, though I never felt confident that I phrased the word correctly, much less understood the meaning. In hindsight, maybe he told me that he was weeping in a

First Revelation

divine language that I had yet to fully understand (the words appeared broken, though that could have been due to my lack of complete knowledge of the language). Perhaps the real answer was "one of two" and that caused him to tear up from either my naiveté to my role or possibly due to a higher-than-expected level of understanding in how to ask that particular question in humility. Though I received a direct answer, I still have questions remaining in the interpretation.

As we ended that series of questions, I was cognizant that I did not want to take his attention away from everyone else. I was already extremely thankful that I had received answers to questions – and that this experience was as clear as it had been. I looked around the group of people. They were all intrigued with the elder. He was clearly our teacher. I noticed Bryan was standing in the group and one other person I knew, but could not identify. As we stood there, a man walked up whom I instantly recognized. I was still filled with such child-like excitement. I reached out with both hands and grabbed his left hand as I said, "Hey [his name that I was not allowed to bring back with me]. Let me introduce you. This is Jesus." I was cutoff as soon as I began to say his name (I was making sure to pronounce it hay-zoose).

As I was cutoff, I realized I was being corrected. I was not saying his correct name. The elder said, "Samson. I am Samson." He looked down at me and smiled. I was extremely embarrassed, but I also felt forgiveness and understanding on not being able to recall his name. He laughed and carried on shaking the hand of the man I introduced him to. After the

Rebirth I

introduction, Samson said we should all follow him to sing. We walked about ten yards from the place we were standing and circled around and sat upon a great chariot. There were no horses attached, but I can only describe the seats and the object as a chariot. Samson stood in the middle of the group. I was on his right, furthest away from him. Bryan was on his left – approximately two or three people removed.

Samson told us the name of the song we were about to sing and he started singing. His voice was pure and clear. All of the others immediately began to sing and the energy rose up through our group. I could not recall the words to the song, as I was lost in awe of the sound of the voices. Samson continued to make eye contact with just me in the group. It was as if he knew I was entirely lucid in the experience and wanted me to know that I knew he knew. His gaze was overpowering – and honestly, very awkward. Everyone around us was also aware of the gaze, making it increasingly more awkward – regardless of how awkward it was in the beginning.

It is one thing to have the gaze of "the girl" stare deep into your soul. It is another to have a man do the same thing. It was enough for me to avert eye contact because his eyes penetrated deeper into my soul than anyone else I had experienced in Heaven aside from "the girl." And honestly, the circumstance of it made me very uncomfortable because the gaze came from a man – though I know 100% that it was a gaze of Agape, and not anything sexually related. This was just the first time in a Heavenly setting that I had experienced this, and honestly – it will take some getting used to mentally.

First Revelation

Overall, this means several things: (1) Agape is unconditional Love for another regardless of gender. (2) Agape has nothing to do with the feeling of "Love for another or a brother" in earthly terms. (3) Agape has nothing sexually related attached to the concept. (4) If nothing is based on sexual drive, then I am left to ponder if/how sexual drive exists in The Heaven. (5) The experience of agape from the same gender in a vision could be related to the misunderstanding of homosexuality on Earth – meaning, the experience of agape could cause a person to desire to seek out that same feeling from an earthly counterpart, thus breaking the gender laws that God has placed on Earth. It could be seen as misinterpretation of a divine concept.

So anyway – I digressed for a moment, but these are all thoughts that were going through my head as everyone was singing. The words to the song sounded like they were in Latin or possibly Austrian, though I was interpreting them in English. The song continued to repeat the words, "Beautiful Blue Eyes" among other Latin words. The song was simple and elegant – much like a lullaby. As I glanced down and away from Samson's gaze, I told him I did not remember the words to the song. A girl sitting to my left glanced up at me. She had auburn hair and was holding a piece of papyrus that contained the lyrics. She held it out in front of both of us so I could follow along. I began to sing. Then I awoke.

...

After the experience, I researched descriptions of Heaven from the Bible. The first verses I was directed to was Revela-

Rebirth I

tion 7:13-17. As I read the passage, it struck a chord with me that caused me want to read all of Revelation 7. Aside from the numeric symbolism, more would unfold. In the beginning verses of Chapter 7, it discusses the four winds. Over the last several days of reading De Architectura by Vitruvius, my vision with the black man, Bryan's visions with the black man, the Enya discussion, I have had continued thoughts on the four winds. Not that I have been able to glean too much from all of the references, but the 8-sphere cube and the eight total winds are definitely all related. The fact that Revelation 7 related not only just to Heaven, the white robes I have been seeing, the 144,000 saved, but it also related to the four winds – which up until now has been an academic study in theology and physics. I am sure there is information to continue to be learned from these concepts.

...

Initially, I wrote the analysis above on the following day of the experience. And while I will not add to or remove from any of the words I wrote so the world may know how it all came to be, I do need/want to emphasize the most important aspect of the experience that I somehow missed as the wonders and splendor of The Heaven captured every bit of my attention. The most important line I missed is when the angel replied, "They are one of two" and everything surrounding that question in the conversation. It is the first time it was identified to me, but it would not be until almost a year later that those words would hold the gravity they hold today as I now understand "what I am" and the role I am to play in

First Revelation

these final days. This was the group of candidates. I was one of them. I am one of them. And in the end, the role we each play will all be revealed as we stand in the presence of our Father.

Requisition

This book was just the beginning. While it covers the longest period of time compared to the other books in the series, it also carries the least detail or explanation of understanding of the experiences. Asking a child to describe what attending a baseball game is like versus asking an adult to describe the experience produces enormous differences in detail. A child is caught up in the luster of the idea of the game. An adult scrutinizes every detail, every nuance. From the architecture of the park, to the price of the tickets, to the differences in jerseys from year to year, changes in the facility, the smells and aromas of the vending stations and the minor details of the attendees surrounding them – the adult can filter through the senses and paint a more precise picture of the experience. So, while this book may have seemed scattered, rest assured this was only the beginning of a grand story to betold. No other writings in the history of mankind have described in detail the origin of how a relationship with God is found. That place in the written word is reserved for this story, His story, the journey leading to Him.

Though this is not the first origin story that has ever taken place throughout the ages, it is the first origin story that has been documented from the point of a spiritual rebirth's im-

Rebirth I

maculate conception. Perhaps in the past, a story to support the present would have caused doubt. But through these words, it shall be revealed how the understanding of the language of the Divine is found. For the Age of Enlightenment is upon those who hear these words, and seek an intimate relationship with God. And for the others, this book must serve as an ark to carry His message through the ages ahead. For these words precede the end of a great cycle – a point in time where only those worthy to ascend will be taken, and those who are not shall be left behind. This is the dawn of Revelation and the drawing to an end of His harvest cycle, where everlasting life is awaiting those who are bound in His Grace.

...
*From generations and generations to come,
this is the revelation of God's grand unveiling.*
...

www.ingramcontent.com/pod-product-compliance
Lightning Source LLC
Chambersburg PA
CBHW021141080526
44588CB00008B/156